Making a World of Difference of Difference One Quilt at a Time

MAKING A WORLD
OF DIFFERENCE
ONE QUILT AT A TIME

*Inspiring Stories about Quilters
& How They Have Touched Lives*

RUTH McHANEY DANNER

New World Library
Novato, California

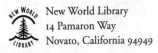 New World Library
14 Pamaron Way
Novato, California 94949

Text design by Tona Pearce Myers

Library of Congress Cataloging-in-Publication Data
Danner, Ruth McHaney, author.
Making a world of difference one quilt at a time : inspiring stories about quilters and how they have touched lives / Ruth McHaney Danner.
    pages   cm
Includes index.
ISBN 978-1-60868-344-4 (paperback) — ISBN 978-1-60868-345-1 (ebook)
1. Charities. 2. Charities—United States. 3. Quilters—Biography. 4. Quilters—United States—Biography. I. Title.
HV27.D36 2015
361'.05—dc23   2015027214

First printing, November 2015
ISBN 978-1-60868-344-4
Printed in the USA on 100% postconsumer-waste recycled paper

10   9   8   7   6   5   4   3   2   1

To Mark Danner, my husband of thirty-nine years,
who painstakingly searches for dropped needles,
puts up with a quilt frame that invades our living space,
and still manages to love quilts as much as I do

Contents

3. FAR-FLUNG QUILTING

4. SPREADING THE COMFORT, KEEPING THE FAITH

5. COMFORT AT BEGINNING AND END

6. Scholarly Workers

7. Bringing Comfort
When Disaster Strikes

INTRODUCTION

What do quilters look like? A grandma in a rocking chair, with a thimble on her finger? Elderly ladies perched around a quilting frame, stitching and chatting?

Although some people still fit these traditional images, many others go far beyond. Today's quilters, young and old, lead busy lives. They have jobs outside the home in addition to family responsibilities. Somehow, during the kids' soccer practice, at a lunch break, or late at night, they find time to add a few stitches to their newest creation.

Amazingly, they also find time to give away those creations once they're finished.

This book presents quilters who do just that. The people featured here represent countless others, all of whom donate their skills to the benefit of humankind. Some do so with scrappy utility quilts, and some with dazzling works of art. Some make small-scale quilts; others go grand. Some do their quilting while the public looks on, and others remain anonymous.

While writing and interviewing, I came across several quilters and quilt lovers whose donations benefit various charities, but who did not want recognition. I raise my thimble in salute to them:

- Two Texas women who have, over many years, stitched beautiful quilts for young mothers graduating from a drug-rehab program.
- An Arkansas mother who, after tragically losing

two sons, channeled her grief into quilts. Out of her own pocket, she secretly paid a year's rent on a meeting room for her fledgling quilt group.

- A woman in Nebraska whose apartment serves as an unofficial home for runaways. She welcomes occasional wayward youths for a night or two, then sends them on their way — each with a new quilt.
- A family who paid $325 for a baby quilt at an auction. The quilt itself, stitched by a good-hearted donor, might have been worth a third of that amount. Still, the family raised their bid again and again, knowing their donation would help to fund a scholarship at a small private university.
- Members of a New York quilt guild who regularly give a stack of quilts to a women's center specializing in rape recovery.
- A Massachusetts woman who organized friends to make quilts for all people injured at the Boston Marathon bombing in 2013.
- A prominent author of quilt-themed novels who donates the proceeds from her speaking engagements to literacy programs and scholarships for librarians.
- A small group in Indiana that makes quilts for all the members of each family receiving a Habitat for Humanity house in their county.

In all these cases, as well as the ones chronicled in this book, people give of themselves willingly. Why?

Reasons vary. Arkansas quilter Deena Hutchinson Flannigan says, "It's for the love of quilting!" She's right. If quilters didn't enjoy the planning, cutting, piecing, and layering, they'd move on to knitting, cross-stitch, or other handicraft.

They also do it for the love of giving. Many of the people interviewed for this book indicated their joy in making and donating quilted creations. "I usually give my quilts away," says Louisiana resident Barrett Beasley. California quilter Jane Cain adds, "You can only have so many quilts at your own house!" To them, stockpiling quilts in a closet holds no joy, but passing them along provides great satisfaction.

Another reason for making quilts involves a spiritual component, understood only by like-minded individuals. Gracie Campbell, who's lived around the country and has joined the local quilt guild in every new hometown, says, "When I feel unrest in my soul, I can find peace when I quilt. I guess you could say quilting is a hobby, but I feel it is more than that. It is my therapy."

And there's one more reason they stitch and donate quilts: they believe they're touching someone's life. Indeed, quilters around the world have discovered hundreds of avenues of service while honing their skills. Through these avenues, quilters show not only their needlework skills, but also their creative imaginations. For example, Jane Cain's church group makes lap quilts for cancer patients, delivering each quilt with a matching, fabric-bound journal. In another example, a group makes doll quilts for preschoolers. In yet a third, women stitch patchwork Christmas stockings, which are given and regiven to raise money for various charities.

Raising money, raising awareness, raising hopes — a quilt can accomplish any or all of these. When given to a poverty-stricken child in India, an aging veteran in Missouri, or a premature baby in Georgia, the quilt speaks of love. When donated to a scholarship auction in Arkansas or to a leukemia hospital in Australia, the quilt speaks of concern. And when stitched for an individual suffering a life-threatening ailment, the quilt speaks of compassion and understanding.

So what do quilters look like? They might be grandmas showing love, busy moms expressing concern, or teenagers exhibiting compassion and understanding. All are typical of the people you'll find as you turn the pages of this book. I invite you to enjoy these true stories of quilts and quilters who use their talents to benefit others.

Each section presents a specific theme, and at the conclusion of every story you'll find a "Binding Stitch" paragraph. Quilters know that the binding — the strip of fabric sewn along the perimeter to finish the quilt — can be added by machine or by hand. In either case, the stitches represent the end of the job. While quilters are sewing on their bindings, they're usually thinking of their next project. Likewise, the "Binding Stitch" in this book will signal the end of the story. As a bonus, it will also offer ideas for you to start a project of your own. You can also get more information about the story you've just read by researching online. Please realize the links and websites provided were accurate at the time of printing; some may have changed by the time you read this book. In those cases, you can utilize your own search engine to dig deeper. As you do, perhaps you'll find encouragement and inspiration to use your skills and resources to touch lives in your world.

COMFORTING
THE CHILDREN

Want to start a community quilting group? Try old-school publicity.

That's what Virginia Biela and her friends did in White Settlement, Texas. Instead of today's electronic social media, these women used supermarket bulletin boards and wrote a brief article for the local newspaper. With a whoosh, Virginia's group took off, thanks to an initial donation of "a whole room full of material," she recalls. "We brought five carloads of fabric from one donor's house."

The old-fashioned notices also garnered several volunteers. "We got people who couldn't sew, but we could still use them. There's a job for anybody." Indeed, she can find a place for every willing hand — sorting fabric, cutting, ironing, or layering quilt tops with batting and backing.

And what's the goal of all this volunteering? Project Linus.

Named after Charles Schultz's *Peanuts* comic-strip character who always carried his security blanket, Project Linus began in 1995. Since then, this nonprofit organization has established chapters in all fifty states in order to provide blankets or quilts to children in need. Project Linus volunteers like Virginia donate an astounding 350 bedcovers to children every month.

The personal touch of these simple quilts and blankets can make a huge impact on their recipients. Carol Babbitt, president of the national Project Linus organization, says on the group's website, "The comfort brought to a child by a Project Linus security blanket should not be underestimated.

Thanks to our many blanketeers and our chapter coordinators, millions of children and their families have been given comfort and security at a time when they need it most. In addition, blanketeers are given an opportunity to use their talents and abilities in a most rewarding way."

Virginia Biela has seen that reward within her group. She recalls, for example, two young quilters in separate meetings with Project Linus workers. "We had a ten-year-old. Her mother brought her in, and she sat in a corner, working for three hours. She made a quilt all by herself!" With a smile, she says the girl gained confidence and a new set of skills. Likewise, Virginia remembers another girl who came to meetings with her grandmother. This young teen took scraps home, designed her own quilt top, and then sewed it together herself. Her eagerness and enthusiasm encouraged her fellow Project Linus workers.

Like these girls, Virginia started quilting as a child. "I grew up with Mother, aunts, neighbors — all did quilts out of scraps, like overalls and shirts. I slept under a quilting frame, hooked to the ceiling." She learned sewing from her mother at the treadle machine, and when Virginia reached high school, she gravitated toward home economics and sewing classes.

While engaged to be married, she watched her mother make a basket quilt, which became her wedding gift in 1950. But the young bride herself didn't find much time for quilting. "After I got married," she says, "I had three children. My husband rented a sewing machine for me to make maternity clothes." He eventually bought that Singer for her, and she still has it, more than sixty years later.

After several decades, Virginia's interest in quilting got new life when her widowed mother moved in. "She came, along with her quilt patterns, quilt scraps, quilt frames. This kept her busy. We set the frames up for her. I started making quilt tops, and we quilted together."

Now she's constantly involved in this hobby. "I make queen-size quilts for all family members on their fiftieth wedding anniversary," she says. "I also make a quilt for every grandchild." In 2006 she heard about Project Linus, though she'd volunteered as a blanketeer for its predecessor, ABC Quilts. She liked the Linus philosophy and soon organized a group at Bethany Christian Church in White Settlement, serving thereafter as project coordinator. She also participates in another Linus group at a church in nearby Benbrook, where she holds the office of treasurer. Her Linus groups donate quilts to numerous charities in Tarrant County: AIDS Outreach, Catholic Charities for Abused and Neglected Children, Child Protective Services, and The Warm Place, which offers grief counseling for children.

One of Virginia's favorite aspects of Linus involves meeting the recipients. In many situations, because of confidentiality issues, that's not possible. However, she notes one prominent exception. "Twice a year," she says, "Cook Children's Hospital hosts us. They treat us to valet parking and a free lunch." Although those perks garner smiles, Virginia admits the real joy comes from seeing the youngsters. "The children get to come

Virginia Biela poses with some of the Linus quilts she and her group have produced.

down out of their hospital rooms with their IV poles. They get to pick out their own quilts." Their enthusiastic giggles thrill the quilters' hearts, she says. On some occasions, the hospital even allows Linus volunteers to visit the neonatal intensive care unit (NICU) and observe firsthand how their baby quilts are used.

A person who doesn't quilt might not get it: how a simple bedcover — 36 inches square or larger, tied with crochet thread — serves as a bridge between generations and brings joy to maker and recipient. Just ask Virginia and members of her Linus groups, whose old-school publicity gets results. Or ask the children who get the quilts. They'll all give the same answer: it's the personal touch.

Binding Stitch

If you live in the Dallas–Fort Worth area, you can learn more about volunteer opportunities at Cook Children's Hospital; see www.cookchildrens.org. Project Linus volunteers include people who quilt, crochet, and knit. Get involved and use your skills to help children! Look for a chapter in your area at www.projectlinus.org. Besides official Linus chapters, scores of quilting guilds around the country donate to Project Linus. Among them is Union County Night Owls Quilt Guild in southern Arkansas. This guild (with fewer than fifty members) has made numerous bedcovers for charities, including over three thousand quilts for Linus since 2007, according to member Trisha Nash.

Photo on page 4 courtesy of Virginia Biela.

A Special Nursery

Dad's patience is wearing thin. His wife's in the hospital after surgery, and he's caring for twin sons less than a year old. Changing diapers, warming formula, getting up at all hours, squeezing in hospital visits — all have taken a toll on his mental and emotional well-being. When will he have time to get a haircut and follow up on those job applications he's been submitting?

Across town, a single mom, depressed and prone to drug abuse and self-mutilation, glances at her three-year-old and crawls back into bed. Maybe the child will be all right for a couple of hours while she sleeps.

In yet another home, a mom and dad are fighting again. They say they love each other but can't seem to agree on anything. Even simple chores, like taking out the trash and washing the dishes, trigger another episode. Meanwhile, their preschool daughter listens from the next room and makes herself small behind the family's tattered sofa.

What's a child to do? What's a parent to do? Where can they find help before the problems get worse? Call the crisis nursery.

When we think of the word "nursery," an image of babies in cribs or toddlers in swing sets might come to mind. Or we think of a day care with laughing preschoolers digging in the sandbox. But there's another kind of nursery. Sure, it has all of those components — and more. Even the name gives a clue: crisis nursery.

This special place is a facility that provides short-term care to newborns through six-year-olds, protecting them from situations that could lead to incidences of abuse or neglect.

What kinds of parents put children in a crisis nursery? Parents who love their little ones enough to ask for help.

The Vanessa Behan Crisis Nursery in Spokane, Washington, is a great example. Since its beginnings in 1987, it has welcomed an average of four thousand children a year, providing residential care for preschoolers for up to seventy-two hours. It also offers support for parents: crisis counseling, referrals to social-service agencies, parenting classes, and family-support groups.

Moreover, it does all this with a nonjudgmental attitude, realizing that some adults face overwhelming odds in their lives. They may not have the emotional reserves or the physical resources to cope with their problems. In fact, personal issues, such as low self-esteem and social isolation, can escalate to crisis levels for these folks. Substance abuse, homelessness, and even inappropriate expectations can also balloon out of control if not handled properly. But with the right kind of support, parents in these circumstances often find the strength to build positive lives for themselves and their children.

Vanessa Behan Crisis Nursery accomplishes this goal through private donations. A whopping 100 percent of the facility's budget comes from contributions from individuals, corporations, service organizations, foundations, trusts, and fund-raising events. In addition, a multitude of volunteers serve as helpers in child care, yard care, janitorial service, and building maintenance.

But money and volunteer hours aren't the only donations welcomed at Vanessa Behan. The nursery also appreciates gifts from individuals and merchants in the community: diapers, baby wipes, toilet paper, trash bags, kitchen supplies, nonperishable foods, baby food, and formula. And quilts.

Celia Benzel coordinates Charity Central, an arm of the Washington State Quilters (WSQ). She works with dozens of WSQ members who piece and quilt for a variety of charities, and one of their favorites is the Vanessa Behan Crisis Nursery. Every three months, Celia carries an armload of quilts to the center. Dora the Explorer, Spiderman, ballerinas, and fire trucks cavort in patterns of pinwheels, rail fences, and simple squares on the 150 quilts she brings annually. She believes that each quilt in her arms has been "made for somebody who's going to love it and appreciate it and use it."

In her imagination, she can even picture the kids' reaction. "I know the faces of the children when they see these quilts. It's just going to bring them a moment of pure joy."

Vanessa Behan's executive director, Amy Knapton, agrees. In an interview with a local television station, she says, "Kids can kind of shut out the world by hiding in a blanket, if they want to. The quilt is something that hopefully will remind them of their experience here, that they found warmth and love and nurturing here."

A couple of those quilts will go home with the twins, after their harried father has twenty-four hours to rest and regroup. Another quilt will comfort the three-year-old whose mother will consider getting help for her personal problems. Yet another will be cuddled by a preschooler who may no longer have reason to fear her parents' angry outbursts.

When adults recognize they need help, they'll find it at the crisis nursery. Their children, meanwhile, find shelter, a comfortable bed, and a colorful quilt to make their lives a little brighter.

Binding Stitch

There's probably a facility in your area like Vanessa Behan. Just type "crisis nursery" and your state name into your search engine, and you'll discover many ways to help. If you live in eastern Washington, check out the Behan nursery at www.vanessabehan.org.

Getting a Head Start

You won't find the word "quilter" among the list of volunteers needed on Head Start's webpage. But you will find other, seemingly more practical categories, such as bathroom helper, field-trip aide, and kitchen assistant.

No matter. The Mississippi Valley Quilters Guild (MVQG) has found a way to serve Head Start by making and donating a special gift to each student.

The MVQG holds meetings in Moline, Illinois, but its membership spans the Quad Cities, which, in addition to Moline itself, include Davenport and Bettendorf, Iowa, and Rock Island and East Moline, Illinois. The combined population of these five cities — when the fifth was added the "Quad" label remained — is almost four hundred thousand, on both sides of the Mississippi River. That means the guild has found countless ways to help a large community of suffering and needy people.

The guild makes quillos for one of its charity projects; they're a combination quilt and pillow. A quick seamstress can make a couple of them in a few hours, and they're donated to Hope Lodge, a temporary residence for patients receiving cancer treatments through the University of Iowa hospital system.

Another group within MVQG makes quilts for Habitat for Humanity in the Quad Cities. According to president Nancy Jacobsen, "This is a loose organization in our guild. We distribute at least one quilt to each family when they take over ownership of their new home." Sometimes, she says, families receive more than one quilt, depending on the needs of their members. In one year recently, the guild gave quilts to five Habitat families in Illinois and Iowa.

Smaller, lesser-known charities get attention from MVQG as well: a long-term care center and an adult day care both get lap robes; the Salvation Army Family Services and the Women's Choice Center get quilts for residents' beds; a shelter for abused women and children gets quilts and other bedding. The guild has designated each February as Charity Sewing Month. During its two meetings that month, members construct quilt tops for many of these agencies.

And then there's Head Start. Across the United States, Head Start operates as a school-readiness and family-support program. It provides an array of comprehensive services at no cost to low-income families of preschoolers. The program focuses on children with health-related problems and disabilities, working to connect them to assistance and medical services. It also tries to promote each child's self-concept and reinforce good patterns of behavior. In every community — including Moline and East Moline — it helps hundreds of children and their parents. Head Start receives funds from the Department of Health and Human Services and the Department of Agriculture, but it still solicits donations and volunteer assistance on the local level.

So MVQG members have slipped in under the radar to serve the children of Head Start in an unexpected way: by making a doll quilt for each boy and girl. Every December since 1995, the guild distributes a thousand of these little quilts. Nancy says most of them are 24-inch squares, with

Mississippi Valley quilter Margaret Paulos shows one of the doll quilts made for Head Start students in Iowa's Quad Cities.

bright colors and child-friendly prints acceptable to youngsters from various ethnic backgrounds. She herself stitches up scores of doll quilts each year, using fabrics especially for children. "I make sort of an 'I Spy' quilt that parents can use to interact with their child," she says.

Because the quilts are given to all Head Start preschoolers, the guild asks quilters to include little-boy themes on half of their quilts. "After all," Nancy notes, "many of the boys will need nurturing skills as adults," and quilts can help encourage that.

Guild members donate fabric for these quilts, and the guild buys batting. A committee within MVQG meets monthly to make forty to fifty quilt tops and then create ready-to-quilt kits. Each kit includes top, batting, and backing, placed in a recycled plastic bag that once held a newspaper. At the guild's next general meeting, members pick up one or more bagged kits to take home and complete.

When Head Start preschoolers receive the finished doll quilts, they realize strangers did something special for them. They may face struggles in life, but they have a doll quilt to remind them of caring people.

And those caring people in the Mississippi Valley Quilt Guild will continue making doll quilts, quillos, lap robes, and many more quilts. Why? The population of Quad Cities — including families and individuals struggling with a variety of issues — demands it. Nancy Jacobsen explains by quoting one of the group's avid volunteers: "The need for charity exists because people are suffering."

Binding Stitch

The Mississippi Valley Quilt Guild has photos and other information at www.mvqg.org. You might also want to check out the Quad Cities Head Start program (www.projectnow.org/headstart.htm) and then see what's available in your own community.

Photo on page 12 courtesy of Nancy Jacobsen.

Linda Arye believes the old saying "One person's trash is another's treasure."

Back in 2000, she recalls, she visited the Philadelphia Design Center and "noticed numerous industrial-size trash bags filled with discontinued designer fabric that were to be thrown away." She asked if she could have that fabric, though she had no idea at the time what she might do with it. She simply wanted to save it from a landfill.

Then she thought of an earlier experience. "I remembered a time when my daughter, Mollie, was hospitalized and not allowed to have her 'bear-bear' to hold on to." Even then, Linda wondered if an all-cotton, washable quilt would have been acceptable to hospital staff. Surely, she thought, a quilt "would have made the experience less frightening."

She talked about her plan to use those scraps to make and donate a few children's quilts, but she didn't get the response she wanted. "I was assured by all my friends and family that this was a dumb idea, and no one would make quilts for strangers' children — and do it for free!"

That didn't stop her, though. She continued asking a growing circle of acquaintances and finally got a positive response. Quilts for Kids, Inc. (QFK), took off and has been going strong for fourteen years. Now she encourages those who do indeed make quilts for strangers' children: "You have managed to help me prove those naysayers wrong.

You have given from your hearts and helped to turn tears into smiles for tens of thousands of children you never even knew existed."

To kids who suffer from abuse or from a life-threatening ailment, such as AIDS or cancer, QFK donates thirty thousand quilts annually. That outlandish number is possible thanks in part to QFK's one hundred chapters and their volunteers.

Besides this army of willing workers, Linda says she gets assistance from corporate sponsors. For example, Procter & Gamble's Downy Touch of Comfort program has helped send ten thousand kits to quilters across the country, who stitch and quilt and bind them into useable bedcovers. Another sponsor, Dominion Energy, provides grants to fund workshops. A variety of textile companies contribute money, and Rotary International gives matching grants to purchase fabric, since the scrap donations can no longer fill the need.

Even more amazing: Linda says many professionals in the design industry "have sent us fabrics, created fabric lines in support of Quilts for Kids, and lowered prices so we have greater buying power." Donations large and small allow Linda to purchase popular, kid-friendly fabrics and to ship quilts to children's hospitals throughout North America. QFK, Linda says, "combines purchased fabrics with the donated fabric, which we still keep from landfills, and creates beautiful quilts for children."

Because hospitals have strict guidelines, these quilts must contain only new, 100 percent cotton. If quilters use flannel, it must be a high-quality fabric that washes well and does not pill. In addition, QFK cannot accept donations of repurposed materials, such as T-shirts, pajamas, sheets, or curtains, because of immunity issues at hospitals. Quilts must be machine-quilted every two inches in order to withstand numerous washings and dryings in industrial machines. Batting should be low-loft cotton, polyester, or a cotton-poly combination.

The finished quilts, about 40 by 45 inches, must travel to the QFK headquarters in Pennsylvania to be inspected and labeled. Then they will be distributed as needed across the country. If a quilter prefers to keep her donation closer to home, she may contact the nearest QFK chapter for instructions.

Arriving by the hundreds, these donations are processed and sent to children in need — like a girl named Faith. In a video, Faith and her mother sit together. Mom speaks first, explaining that Faith's condition at age four was life-threatening. "She'd been in a very, very serious accident. She almost died. She had to be medevacked from where we were to a hospital that handles trauma for children. She was frightened by all the bright lights and the noise." A kind nurse took notice and pulled a quilt out of a nearby cabinet.

At this point, Faith, now a teen, picks up the story. "She wrapped me in it and said, 'Now you're gonna be safe,' and I immediately stopped crying. I felt like someone was hugging me. It was really cool."

Other families have seen similar results. One dad's thank-you note describes the moment before his daughter was taken into surgery: "They wrapped the quilt around her and told her that it was a magic quilt that has made her a princess. She stopped crying, started smiling, and began to laugh with the nurses. The whole atmosphere changed as they wheeled her away to the operating room." That grateful father believes the "magic" is the love from the quilt makers. "Quilts for Kids," he asserts, "was able to comfort my child when I could not physically be there with her."

Another example comes from Stephanie Loveridge, unit manager of Child and Adolescent Psychiatry at Virginia Baptist Hospital. She says, "When children arrive at our unit, they are usually either physically aggressive or 'shut down' and saying nothing. Many are scared to be away from their caregivers…especially on the child's first night with us. It's very traumatic. But your quilts have helped immensely in easing their transition."

She describes dramatic individual cases, such as the suicidal eight-year-old who couldn't calm down until he received a quilt. He loved the fabric with cars, and he immediately settled into his room. In another incident, the unit received a child "from the coal mines of southwest Virginia. She came with shoes that had holes in them and no socks and was extremely dirty." After giving her a bath and a lice treatment, the staff took her to a room with stacks of quilts. "When she got to pick out her quilt, she literally welled up with tears of joy. At home, she was sleeping on a mattress on the floor with her siblings, and they all shared one lightweight sheet. She was thrilled to have her quilt on her very own hospital bed."

Nurse Loveridge concludes with heaps of praise for QFK. "Your quilts and your service in making them are a part of our children's journey to emotional and mental healing. Thank you for your service!"

That's what Linda Arye and her hundreds of volunteer

quilters like to hear. Those bags of discarded fabric have been multiplied and transformed into countless quilts of comfort. "If we can lessen the suffering of children by showing them that they are loved, then we have reached our goal," Linda says.

Binding Stitch

QFK is a nonprofit organization and appreciates donations. Linda says, "Please visit www.quiltsforkids.org, and remember to add us to your United Way program (Southeast PA 47897)." For detailed instructions for making a quilt, see the FAQ tab of the website.

Children at risk. The very phrase conjures up negative images: little ones snatched from their beds by police during a late-night drug raid; young victims of abuse with bruises and broken bones; babies with physical, mental, or emotional damage due to their mothers' unhealthy lifestyles.

But less traumatic pictures emerge as well, including youngsters mired in poverty and sight-impaired toddlers. All these images present a sense of hopelessness, but we must not despair. There is hope — even in the bleakest situations — thanks to various social services, and thanks to quilts.

Quilters in western Oregon have found a way to help their community while honing their craft. Quilts from Caring Hands (QCH), a 501(c)(3) nonprofit, provides opportunities for quilters to connect with a variety of social-service groups. In each case, the connection offers benefits to many.

For example, children at the pediatric chemotherapy unit of Good Samaritan Hospital get bright, kid-size quilts when they come in for treatments. Nearby, special-needs youngsters receive quilts and tactile lap aprons at Randall Children's Hospital. And visually impaired kids throughout the area's public schools can run their hands over quilts made with fake fur, rickrack, and other materials that beg to be touched.

QCH appreciates donations of cash, of course, but nonmonetary gifts bring smiles as well. For example, the organization says, "We love receiving donations of UFOs [unfinished objects], because whatever work the donor has finished is work that we do not have to do." Quilting volunteers set these UFOs together into original, nontraditional quilt tops. Even a few odd blocks can be creatively joined to make a crib-size quilt. The quilters also appreciate donations of time. Nonsewers as well as expert needleworkers can find a place in the group.

QCH donates over five hundred quilts annually to its chosen charities. Included among its beneficiaries is the Parent Enhancement Program (PEP). Volunteers there try to nurture, educate, and inspire parents and parents-to-be, ages thirteen to twenty-five, who might otherwise fall into unwise habits and lifestyles. PEP promotes "the well-being and self-sufficiency of young parents and their children, through wrap-around services which support a healthy pregnancy, healthy children, and the well-being of the whole family." PEP hopes to show young parents how to be successful persons, capable of leading strong families. The organization's success is due to its staff of dedicated volunteers committed to preventing child abuse.

Teen parents face a variety of challenges, including lack of support from their families of origin. In some cases, the teens are booted out of their homes; in other cases they stay but receive little help or compassion. Their sense of self-worth plummets. But assistance from the Parent Enhancement Program — along with a quilt from QCH — can do wonders. Susan Hirsch, of PEP, says, "Something nice and new such as one of your quilts is a real boost to a teen parent's self-esteem."

Another beneficiary of these quilters is the local Center

Against Rape and Domestic Violence (CARDV). This vital service offers help and safety to victims of abuse. One recent survivor of sexual assault says, "CARDV has been a continuing support in my life since leaving my abuser. I wouldn't be where I am now without their constant support." Each year in the Corvallis area, almost two hundred women and children seek CARDV's safe shelter away from abusive situations. This translates into more than two thousand nights in warm beds — all covered with QCH quilts. Mary Zelinka, shelter coordinator, appreciates the quilts and their significance. "For me," she says, "the quilts symbolize a deep respect for each woman and child who comes through our shelter. What a beautiful way to honor survival!"

QCH provides quilts to another unique group: blind and visually impaired children. Called tactile quilts, these creations aren't intended for use as bedding. Instead, they're placed in educational settings, where children can crawl on them, explore various textures, and learn more about the world around them. Each of these quilts has as much textural variety as possible. Fake fur, corduroy, flannel, silks, terrycloth, seersucker, velvet — all find a place in tactile quilts. In addition, QCH encourages volunteers to include bright and bold colors in big zigzags and checks, so that children with limited vision can learn to recognize contrasts.

Kids love these quilts and spend hours studying them with their fingers. Teachers also benefit from QCH's donations. Mary Reid, spokesperson at Marion Education Services District, says, "The quilts have made such an impact on the staff, that they are not alone in caring. There is someone else out there who cares with them and in a sense, then, carries part of the load."

Helping to carry the load may be an underappreciated aspect of quilting. Yet QCH volunteers do this regularly, as they make and donate quilts on a quarterly schedule to numerous charities — with the goal of supporting and encouraging families and children. A quilt at a homeless shelter or a safe house or on a classroom floor all speak of sharing the load.

Most of all, to children and families in crisis the quilts speak of hope.

Binding Stitch

Learn more about QCH in Corvallis, Oregon, at www .quiltsfromcaringhands.com. If you live in western Oregon, you can check out the Center Against Rape and Domestic Violence at www.cardv.org. Or research domestic violence services in your own area, and volunteer your quilting skills. Look at quilt photos and examples at www.quiltsfromcaring hands.com/our_quilts/index.html. Want to make a tactile quilt for a sight-impaired child? Read QCH's website instructions first. These quilts must be a certain size, and their blocks must conform to specific standards. Even so, if you've ever wanted to have fun with wild textures and bold colors, this project is worth a try!

HALOS

Alone in the house, Grandma hangs up the phone, collapses onto the sofa, and cries. She cries for the family trauma that has displaced little grandson Jake. She cries for the child, who's facing an upheaval unlike anything he's known before. And she cries for herself, wondering how she'll manage this new responsibility.

No doubt her responsibility looms large. Speaking to the Department of Social Services, she has just agreed to welcome the four-year-old into her home. She looks around in panic as she wipes her eyes. Where will the boy sleep? She's on a fixed income and can't buy a bed for him. What about extra household supplies? Mercy! She'll also need a car seat right away, and boots and a coat for the rainy season. And what about food? Surely a growing preschooler eats! How will she stretch her limited budget to cover all these expenses? Welcome to the world of kinship caregiver.

Thankfully, the grandmother soon learns she isn't alone — Helping and Lending Outreach Support (HALOS) steps in with assistance. While advocating for children, this organization understands the unique needs of a relative who's suddenly thrust into a caregiver role. That's why a large part of the HALOS program involves the practical considerations of a grandparent or other kinship caregiver.

HALOS serves the tricounty area surrounding Charleston, South Carolina. Working on behalf of children and teens, the group focuses on a special brand of client with one thing in common: a troubled home. Causes of the trouble differ: neglect, abuse, or drug use; a traumatic breakup of the family; a debilitating illness or other parental issue. In every case, the youngster must leave home, at least temporarily.

Next comes the critical question of where to go. Grandpa? Friend of the family? Foster care? HALOS believes, in most cases, the best choice is a family member. When a child leaves home because of trauma, he or she will experience fewer problems if moved to a familiar household instead of to a complete stranger's.

The idea of familiarity and continuity brought the Cobblestone Quilters of Charleston into the HALOS picture. Louise Schmidt, Cobblestone's 2014 community-outreach chairperson, says she chose this charity for the guild's year-long project because the group "wanted something different." In previous years the quilters had supported women's shelters and other similar charities. But as she researched, Louise discovered HALOS's mission. She learned that it seeks to keep kids in a stable situation, and she realized quilts could help.

HALOS serves a huge demographic. The estimated population of the Charleston metro area exceeds seven hundred thousand, and it's the fastest-growing city in South Carolina. With so many people, the need for children's advocates and kinship caregivers continually grows. And the need for supplies grows as well. In fact, Louise says HALOS distributes car seats, kitchen and bathroom necessities, linens, diapers, baby wipes, and numerous other items to kinship caregivers. One of HALOS's most significant giveaways is beds — more than four hundred beds and two hundred cribs each year.

Louise says Cobblestone members donate bedcovers once a month, and HALOS bundles a quilt with each bed. This special quilt "goes with the child," Louise explains, whether he or she remains in the kinship home or moves back to the home of origin. The quilt represents stability and continuity in a young person's life. Kids need that, because, according to one grandmother, "The children we care for have been through so much!"

Caregivers, likewise, need an anchor, and HALOS offers practical assistance as well as support groups, conducted with dignity and respect. One woman, taking custody of a granddaughter who'd been a rape victim, expresses her feelings simply: "I was frightened. I was doing this all by myself." But when HALOS offered to help, her attitude changed for the better, and she moved forward in her new role. As another kinship caregiver says, "I found hope, love, and acceptance at HALOS, when the HALOS staff believed in me."

The charity's website says it "gives kinship caregivers the tools they need to feel empowered." In doing so, it also gives the affected children some tools of their own: love, acceptance, stability, and a quilt. That's why Louise and the Cobblestone Quilters chose this organization for their project, and that's why they work hard to keep up with the demand in the burgeoning Charleston area. Louise admits, "We don't have enough quilts for every bed that's donated, but we're working on it!"

Binding Stitch

If you live in South Carolina, please consider helping HALOS in a tangible way. Ongoing needs include twin beds, bunk beds, toddler beds, and cribs in good condition; new car seats; living-room and dining-room furniture, dressers, and chests; and kitchen and bathroom supplies. Some restrictions apply, and you can find those at www .charlestonhalos.org. Or you can make quilts for HALOS through Louise's quilt guild at www.cobblestonequilters .com. If you live elsewhere, contact your social-services office and ask about local needs.

HONOR FOR
THE MILITARY

A PIECE OF HISTORY

Standing in the businessman's office, Catherine Kreter presented a quilt to a father whose son had recently died in Afghanistan. "It's hard," says Catherine, recalling that moment. "It's really hard emotionally." But definitely worth it.

For years, Catherine has quilted professionally with her longarm machine. Most quilters know about longarms, though few can afford the initial expense and the square footage required. This heavy appliance moves along a track, while the person guides it, to quilt a layered bedcover stretched on a room-size frame.

Long before her meeting with that father, Catherine had joined the Citrus Belt Quilters in Redlands, California. There she met Don Beld, who began the Home of the Brave (HOTB) Quilt Project in 2004. Don wanted to honor military men and women who had died while serving in Iraq and Afghanistan. Many other quilt groups have a similar goal, but Don tried something new — by looking back to an old tradition.

He uncovered a little-known page of history involving quilts made during the Civil War to help Union troops. He learned that a mid-1800s organization, the U.S. Sanitary Commission, oversaw conditions at various hospitals and recruited volunteers to contribute sheets, bandages, socks, and other necessities. Sound familiar? This work eventually morphed into the American Red Cross.

Northern women had leaped at the opportunity to

help, contributing all the requested items — and then some. They added as many as four hundred thousand hand-pieced, hand-quilted coverlets in a four-year period. Each quilt measured 48 by 84 inches — the perfect size for a hospital cot.

Sadly, only a handful of those precious quilts have survived until today. Don found one of them displayed in a Redlands library, and he chose the same Album pattern to piece for his first quilt for this project, which he dubbed Home of the Brave.

That's when Catherine stepped up to volunteer her time, her thread, and her longarm for the quilting of Don's bedcover. In the years since then, she's stayed busy with other replica quilts, finding spare moments between paying jobs. "I've done at least two hundred fifty of the HOTB quilts," she says. "I quilt four to six every month." She then sends them back to the people who pieced them, to be bound and finished.

The Home of the Brave Project appeals, she says, because it's a piece of history. Every HOTB quilt uses the same Album pattern, with the same dimensions, as the Civil War originals. The fifteen blocks are square, each with two intersecting diagonal strips placed against a contrasting background. A stripping separates the blocks.

But another aspect makes the project even more distinctive. "Unlike many, we're not a recognized charity," Catherine says. "Don wanted a grassroots movement — no affiliations — just quilters sending their love. We can take donations, but they're not tax deductible." She points out that all piecers and quilters donate time and supplies, with no desire for repayment.

HOTB has expanded into all fifty states and the U.S. possessions; Britain, Germany, and Australia have honorary chapters. Since 2004, more than 6,150 quilts have been delivered to 5,180 families on behalf of 7,240 fallen heroes. Catherine says people continue to make quilts, and loved ones continue to request these historical replicas. She receives gratification through various thank-you notes, she says, quoting a letter from the parents of an Idaho soldier as an example: "Oh, what a fabulous quilt! The history of the pattern and its replica meant so much. War is war, no matter what the century. We will treasure this memorial."

That kind of gratitude spurs Catherine and quilters across the country to continue their work with HOTB. But there's another element that draws many to this program: quilters themselves are comforted as they sew. One example is Barb Shillinger, who has over fifty years of quilting experience. Barb remembers her mother's quilt frame — four boards with strips of cloth attached by thumbtacks. Her mom pinned the layered quilt to the cloth, then used kitchen chairs to support the wooden frame around which the women gathered to quilt.

Many years and many quilts later, Barb heard about the HOTB project through a friend. Coincidentally, she and her family had recently suffered a loss. She says, "Our son Kevin had just died, and I was in deep mourning. The project 'spoke to me' as having meaning. I realized as a grieving parent that I shared the same grief that parents of military casualties did, though my son was not in the service."

Since then, Barb has used quilting as an avenue of comfort. She even delivers the quilts herself if possible. In one instance, she took a quilt top to the school district where the fallen soldier's mother worked. She says, "The top made the rounds to each of the schools, so all the school district employees would have an opportunity to sign it. Then I finished the quilt and brought it back, so her fellow employees could present it to her." In another instance, she made two quilts for a family — one for the soldier's mother and another for the soldier's teenage son. Barb adds, "It was extra sad, because the dog had not recovered from the loss of her owner and wouldn't go inside the mom's home."

Yes, sad stories often accompany the HOTB quilts. That's why some who donate their handiwork simply can't make the actual presentations. Catherine Kreter fits that category. She says watching tears stream down the face of a dignified businessman isn't easy. In fact, it's hard, really hard.

Binding Stitch

Catherine, national coordinator of HOTB quilts, recommends that you find your local Home of the Brave chapter through the project's website or through Citrus Belt Quilters (www.citrusbeltquilters.org). Additionally, you can find photos of numerous HOTB quilts given to fallen heroes from your state at www.homeofthebravequilts.com. If you know of a family who should receive a Civil War replica quilt, contact HOTB through that website.

Honoring a Soldier

Rusty, a former army corporal, served admirably on the USS *Wharton* during World War II, then came home and married. After numerous jobs over the years, he's now fully retired but still enjoys drives through the countryside and occasional weekends in the camper. Otherwise, he stays close to home and to his wife of sixty-eight years.

He's almost ninety, uses a wheelchair, and has poor hearing. But there's one more trip he needed to take recently: a trip to Washington, D.C., to visit the World War II Memorial built to commemorate service members like himself. Thanks to Honor Flight, he made that trip while he was still able. And, thanks to a group of quilters, he took a special gift with him.

Since 2005 Honor Flight has provided transportation for thousands of aging veterans to and from the nation's capital for the express purpose of visiting this memorial. The idea for the project began in the imagination of retired air force captain and physician assistant Earl Morse. While working in a clinic in Springfield, Ohio, Earl saw news reports about the completion of the memorial in 2004. Naturally, the subject became conversation fodder among Earl's World War II veteran patients.

"Do you think you'll ever go see it?" Earl asked several of them, and the answer was always tentative: "Maybe someday, perhaps with a family member or friend." But months later, when Earl asked the same people again, they responded negatively. Too many obstacles stood in the way: cost, physical impairments, lack of traveling companions. But Earl didn't give up. He knew there had to be a way to get those heroes to D.C. to see their memorial.

Coincidentally, Earl was a licensed private pilot and a member of an aero club at Wright-Patterson Air Force Base in Dayton. Late in 2004, Earl asked one of his elderly patients, "Would it be all right if I personally flew you out to D.C., free of charge, to visit your memorial?" The astounded man accepted the offer and burst into tears. A week later Earl posed the same question to another aging vet and received the same grateful response.

The scene repeated itself several times, and Earl realized he couldn't accommodate everyone by himself. At his next aero club meeting, he addressed the 150 members, stating his need for volunteer pilots. His two stipulations? No veteran would pay for the flight, and the pilot himself must escort the vets around D.C. during their one-day stay. Earl's audience reacted with enthusiasm. Eleven pilots — men who had never met those veterans — stepped forward as volunteers. Honor Flight Network was born.

The program quickly mushroomed, and soon the number of veterans exceeded the capacity of volunteer pilots and their small planes. By the end of 2005, 137 veterans and their escorts used commercial flights, which could transport forty to fifty of them at a time. Within a year, commercial flights became the norm.

The Honor Flight Network has transported nearly one hundred thousand veterans to Washington, D.C., since Earl started it in 2005. With 127 hubs in forty-one states, the program works hard to make sure aging vets can visit their memorial. According to Honor Flight's website, approximately eight hundred World War II veterans die each day in the United States. That's why, it says, "We are committed to do all within our power to make their dream a reality."

So Corporal Rusty and his compatriots found themselves early one rainy morning on a bus, surrounded by a convoy of flag-waving motorcycles, making its way to the airport. A couple of hours later, a Southwest Airlines flight carried them, free of charge, to D.C. Several activities during the trip gave the travelers moments of laughter and nostalgia.

During one such in-flight event, a volunteer reached for his overstuffed duffle bag. He unzipped it and pulled out dozens of small quilts. Most were pieced in patriotic colors, and a quilt was offered to every Honor Flight veteran on the trip.

These quilts — 36-inch square lap robes, actually — came from loving hands in the Missouri River Quilt Guild (MRQG) of Jefferson City. The guild needs approximately fifty lap quilts per trip for the four to six flights made each year. It's easy to see how MRQG members stay busy with this project.

Likewise, across the country numerous other guilds and quilt groups make lap quilts for Honor Flight. From quilters in Rock Springs, Wyoming, to quilters in Waterloo County, Iowa; from the Thread Bears Quilters Guild in Syracuse, New York, to the Gold Coast Quilters Guild in Boca Raton, Florida — you'll find countless examples of supporters.

And Corporal Rusty, the Honor Flight vet? Like his counterparts around the country, he appreciates the patriotic-themed lap quilt, which made the trip to D.C. with him. After returning, he and other veterans have precious memories of touring the World War II Memorial, and they keep the quilts as souvenirs of their flight.

Binding Stitch

If you're a quilter, find a local Honor Flight hub and consider making lap robes for those who fly to D.C. Or you may find other ways to support the program. The website stresses that Honor Flight Network is not associated with any companies that charge a fee to veterans for the trip, so do not be confused by look-alikes on the internet. See www.honorflight.org. For great examples of Honor Flight quilts, see the blog http://joanne-everyonedeservesaquilt.blogspot.com/p/honor-flight-quilts.html. You can find how Southwest Airlines helps Honor Flights at www.honorflight.org/programs/tlc.cfm. Learn more about the Missouri River Quilt Guild at www.facebook.com/MissouriRiverQuiltGuild. To see the other charities mentioned, go to the Samaritan Center at www.midmosamaritan.org and Serve, Inc., at www.serveinc.net.

The Army Babies Quilt Project

The website says it best: "A quilt begins with scattered pieces, scattered like members of military families around the world. The finished quilt is the joining of all the pieces to make a whole. Hopefully, soon all our army families will be whole again."

Roberta Cerniglia's words echo in the hearts of thousands of Americans, many of whom have seen firsthand the sacrifices military families have to make. Roberta, who lives in New York's Hudson River Valley, watched her son graduate from West Point in 2004. He then went to aviation school at Fort Rucker, Alabama, and became a Blackhawk pilot.

While he was stationed in Hawaii, she visited him, and they took a trip to the base commissary to shop for groceries. There, she stopped abruptly, seeing something that changed her life — pregnant women, shopping alone, lots of them.

"I wondered if the fathers weren't going to be home when their babies were born," she recalls. How many young mothers would be giving birth alone? How many young soldiers would be on distant shores, concerned for those mothers and newborns? How many army dads wouldn't even see their babies for weeks or months after birth? Most of all, what could Roberta do about any of this?

"I'd retired," says the former English teacher, "and I just started making some simple quilts, tying basic nine-patches." Then she took another step. "I started calling around to some of the bases," but ran into a few snags. "I spent a lot of time on the phone. The hardest part is getting a contact within the military base."

But she didn't give up. After making several nine-patch coverlets and spending countless hours on the phone, she sent her stack of baby quilts to the Tripler Army Medical Center in Oahu. Since then, Roberta has repeated the process for military hospitals and bases around the country. When friends heard of her work, they joined the effort. However, she has never wanted a big quilting organization and resists the temptation to branch out. "Small and simple" has been her motto from the beginning. She gets a few quilts each month from like-minded donors in and around the Hudson Valley and a few others from patriotic quilters around the country. That's enough to keep her program going.

What keeps Roberta herself going is the requests for baby quilts from across the military spectrum. For example, a young sergeant in Afghanistan wrote on behalf of her brother, also serving there. The sergeant was concerned for her sister-in-law back in the States with a new baby. Could Roberta please send her a quilt? In another instance, a mother wrote to say that her son, a soldier, had recently suffered a brain-damaging injury. He had a new baby at home. Doesn't this baby deserve a quilt, even though the dad's no longer on the front lines?

"I sent him one without hesitation," says Roberta.

As the daughter of a twenty-five-year navy submariner, Roberta knows there's a strain in military families. "They probably move three times in five years," she explains.

"Enlisted men don't make a lot of money, so a lot of times families can't be together at the birth of the baby." Fortunately, military neighbors commiserate and often serve as support, bringing cookies and casseroles as well as babysitting and packing boxes for yet another move.

But quilts fill a different purpose for a young mother. Roberta points out, "A baby quilt from somebody they don't know lets these families know that another American is thankful for the sacrifice they're going through."

As the U.S. military presence overseas decreases, Roberta sees a shift in focus for The Army Babies Quilt Project. "I'm retweaking the project," she says, "and may start sending quilts even if the soldiers aren't deployed in a combat zone." If that happens, she might have to ramp up her work and enlist more volunteers. In any case, she will continue to use baby quilts to help unite army families.

When she sends a quilt to a family, she always asks that the recipient read the accompanying poem first, to set the stage for this special gift. Roberta herself wrote the poem, which expresses her heart:

To an Army Mother

by Roberta Cerniglia

I've sewn a quilt for you and baby
because I thought just maybe
something warm would comfort you
and honor you for all you do.

You, who birthed your child alone
with partner, lover, far from home.

What sadness and joy you must have felt that day
with father, a soldier, so far away.

Let the months fly by and give us peace.
May your courage and hope each day increase.

Soon your soldier will be at your side.
A family filled with Army pride.

So wrap your little one in this red, white, and blue,
Army mother, strong and true!

Binding Stitch

If you want to donate your skills to The Army Babies Quilt Project, please contact Roberta first, through her website (www.armybabies.com). While visiting that site, be sure to look at photos of Army Baby quilts and the families who receive them.

QUILTS OF VALOR

"I didn't know anyone cared." That's the most frequent comment from service members, says Catherine Roberts, when they receive Quilts of Valor (QOV).

Catherine established the nonprofit QOV foundation in 2003, with the goal of making quilts to heal and comfort service members who'd been touched by war. You can hear her passion and almost imagine a raised voice and a pointed index finger when she says: "If you want to do more than talk about supporting our troops, I invite you to take up your sewing implements and help make Quilts of Valor, which *do* make a difference on the road to recovery."

Speaking to quilters and longarmers, she continues, "Use your talents to show these brave young men and women how much we appreciate their sacrifice and service with something very American and very tangible — a wartime Quilt of Valor. In doing so, you are catching them in the QOV net of comfort and love and healing."

Quilts of Valor come in a variety of patterns, many with stars, most in the colors gold, red, white, and blue. The finished quilt must be no smaller than 55 by 65 and no larger than 75 by 90 inches. Quilts may be pieced by one person and quilted by another. Or volunteers may piece one or more individual blocks and submit them to QOV, to be assembled into a top and quilted by others. In addition, quilt makers are encouraged to include photo documentation of their assembly process, along with a journal or letter to the service member. The finished quilt and documents are then assembled in a presentation case.

QOV recipients come from a wide cross section of the military, each with his or her unique story. Dorsey Winfree, a stocky Vietnam veteran with graying hair and mustache, explains his experience. One of twelve soldiers in an armored personnel carrier, he recalls the day they worked to secure a hill. "We were hit by an RPG — a rocket-propelled grenade — and there were six of us that were wounded, and the other six died." His voice breaks, and he wipes his nose as he speaks. "Two of 'em were my real close friends. The other four, I never knew their names." Dorsey spent the next six weeks in a military hospital. Then, after more months of duty, he was discharged in 1971.

But going home presented its own set of problems. "My friends, my peers, just didn't get it," he says. "It was like two worlds. There were protestors at the gates." He wanted to talk about his experiences in Vietnam, but he quickly realized no one wanted to listen. "Only other vets, they could relate."

In 2009, almost forty years after Vietnam, Dorsey was invited to a ceremony ostensibly honoring another veteran. But when the presentations began, someone called his name. He came to the front of the assembly and accepted a quilt in the Courthouse Steps pattern. "It was a complete surprise," he says with a smile. "People actually cared." He admits that the public never acknowledged his service, so he says, "This was, by far, the best event anyone has ever done for me."

In a video Dorsey stands at the Vietnam Memorial Wall. "I think of this every day of my life. But it's mellowing as I age. It's not as traumatic as it used to be." Politics aside, he says, "The war is over. You should honor the people."

That's exactly what the QOV foundation seeks to do with every quilt it presents. Its website emphasizes: "We accept our warriors and veterans with open arms and open hearts. One only has to talk to the veterans of previous wars and conflicts to get a glimpse that the profound effects of war never really leave."

A recent example comes through a thank-you note from an air force captain who'd been wounded along with eight others. "We were rescued and brought to a hospital in Germany," he says. "During my hospital stay, I was given a beautiful quilt made by QOV quilters of Galesburg, Illinois." After an internet search, he found an email address and wrote to that group, saying: "I am so touched by this wonderful gift. It was given to me as they were sending some of my buddies home. It was quite an emotional moment, as our group was going their separate ways, but every one of us was wrapped in a quilt sent from home. The quilt was a great comfort to me and a reminder of why we serve."

Quilters understand that comfort. They also understand the pleasure that goes with it. Floridian Sandra Congleton speaks of "our big joy" when describing the QOV presentation ceremonies she's attended in Jackson, New Orleans, and Pensacola. "Many times," she says, "the quilters are able to hand out the quilts themselves to the troops. This almost always means tears on both sides!" A retired graphic artist, Sandra has her hand — and her heart — in every Quilt of Valor that's presented. She makes the QOV labels, which include the name of the quilt, the creator of the pattern, and the names and locations of the piecers and quilters. There's also space for the veteran's name, along with a flag or star graphic.

These labels and quilts speak of courage and sacrifice beyond the grasp of many civilians, but some quilters seem to get it. Ginger Patano, of Spokane, Washington, learned about QOV a few years ago, when she saw photos of soldiers recovering and leaving a military hospital. She noticed something surprising in the photos. "The hospital put quilts on the guys who came out to get in the helicopters. I thought that was really, really wonderful."

She's pieced several Quilts of Valor since then, some from her own stash and some from blocks donated by others. She quilted one on her sewing machine at home, though she prefers to find a longarm partner to do the quilting.

Either way, she'll make more Quilts of Valor, because the need

Many Quilts of Valor sport a patriotic motif.

never ceases. According to founder Catherine Roberts, the number of wounded service members continues to escalate. "I heard a statistic from the *New England Journal of Medicine*, which had an article on troop injuries," she notes. "For every casualty, multiply that number by ten and you will get an approximate number of wounded." Other sources, she says, put the count even higher.

That's why she's passionate about making quilts for

them all. They need the comfort and healing found in a quilt. And they need to know someone cares.

Binding Stitch

Quilts of Valor must be made according to specific guidelines. If you're interested, check out the website (www.qovf .org), video instructions (www.youtube.com/watch?v=N LnrC9yo8tY), and an individual block pattern (www.qovf .org/Pdf_Files/Hearth&Home_BlockPatternREV-2_ Sep_2014.pdf). If you want to watch Dorsey's complete video interview, go to www.qovf.org/content/meat-potatoes .html. To find your local QOV chapter, see www.qovf.org /content/qovf-around-the-world.html.

Photo on page 43 courtesy of Eastern Washington Quilts of Valor.

3

FAR-FLUNG
QUILTING

National Geographic calls them the "Tree-house People," because most of their huts perch on stilts high above the ground. Four thousand men, women, and children of the Korowai tribe build their tree houses in the lowland jungles of southern Papua, Indonesia. One pilot quoted in the *National Geographic* article lands his float plane on a nearby river to deliver supplies. He calls this area "the most remote in an already remote land — about the farthest place from anywhere." And that's where missionaries Trevor and Teresa Johnson, both RNs, have chosen to live with their three young children.

As a child in Missouri, Trevor loved hiking and canoeing, but he never imagined himself serving as a missionary. During his teenage years he saw agnosticism as the only answer to life's perplexing questions. Yet, he says, as an eighteen-year-old he began reading the Bible and gradually came to understand God's claim on his life. That pivotal summer eventually led to a nursing degree and a wife with similar interests in medicine and service.

While on short-term nursing duty in the jungles of the Amazon, Trevor says he sensed a divine calling. "I delivered a baby in a simple shack on the banks of that monstrous water. I cut the umbilical cord with a Wilkerson shaving razor. Dogs lapped up the drippings underneath the floorboards. It was a shocking experience, but life-changing. I realized that my gifts and abilities could either earn a decent wage in America or be the God-ordained difference between life and death for somebody living in a remote region." So they moved to Indonesia to serve as nurses, and now they work under the auspices of Heart Cry Missionary Society.

Certainly, most Americans would consider their situation primitive, though Trevor prefers the term "low-tech." The Johnsons admit that the lack of basic hygiene astounded them — even at an Indonesian hospital. Trevor says, "Imagine our surprise when we witnessed used disposable latex gloves being washed with rubbing alcohol and hung out to dry on a clothesline." He recalls trash and medical waste littering the hallways, and he even saw a rat scurrying along one wall.

What's worse, after arriving in their remote location, they discovered a dire lack of medical knowledge. They found traditional practices that defied American logic: belief that wearing a pair of scissors on a cord around the neck will ward off evil spirits from a pregnant woman, or that delivery can be aided by bathing in seven wells seven times during the seventh month of pregnancy or slipping a live eel down the woman's shirt.

Americans with medical training might respond with shock. They'd be tempted to flaunt their knowledge, charging into the village like gangbusters to show residents how wrong they are. Yet Trevor and Teresa didn't do that. They chose instead to enlarge their worldview, to listen and learn from the culture, to guide gently, and to love their neighbors without an air of superiority. As a result, in the eight years the Johnsons have lived in this village, they've gained respect from a group who would have otherwise shunned them.

How? Trevor says he and Teresa began with basics. "We practice community health preventative measures: boil your water, bathe regularly, and don't poop where you drink." From that starting point, they treat as many maladies as possible in their makeshift clinic. The most serious cases they take to the nearest city, making sure the medical community there does not look down upon the poor villagers.

And poor they are. Residents of some areas of rural Indonesia earn less than $2 per day, but the Korowai have no income whatsoever — except meager government support. With this issue in mind, Trevor and Teresa focus on community health, even as they consider how to help with the practical, economic needs around them. During a hospital visit, Trevor met a Javanese evangelist named Nunu, who made quilts to support his ministry. Women in Nunu's village followed his example, set up a quilting house, and began earning an income. Now, after a few years in the business, they can afford to send their children to school. They've improved their living conditions,

Most of the villagers live in tree houses like this.

which includes buying enough food to keep their families from going to bed hungry.

Even so, quilting is hard work in that village. Women must carry all supplies through the rugged jungle from the road to their unmarked quilting house. After a quilt is completed, they must haul it out again before it can be shipped to its purchaser.

But quilting continues in spite of — or because of — these troubles. Like American quilting bees of yesteryear, the fifteen to twenty women in this group work all day. Some sit at machines, piecing, while others gather around large frames with quilts stretched taut. They sew 10 to 12 stitches per inch and in a week create a dozen beautiful bedcovers in patterns like Lone Star, Snowball, and Trip around the World. Each queen-size quilt, Trevor estimates, gives work to ten women for ten days. They also make smaller items, such as baby quilts, Christmas tree skirts, and table runners. All sell at reasonable prices.

Trevor says buying one of the group's quilts is not simply a donation to the poor. "This is more like an investment that is self-sustaining. All profits broaden or sustain the existing network of gainfully employed women, providing them with a wage that will allow them to sustain their families, while preserving the biblical work ethic." He likens the process to the microloan system. The money earned goes back to the women, so they may produce more quilts and thus earn more money. Even better, the quilting jobs lend dignity to women who would otherwise languish in poverty.

The Johnsons, who visit Nunu's village annually, have seen the quality of life improve there, thanks in part to the women's newfound status in the community. Women have discovered that quilts can upgrade their homes and educate their children, while raising the whole village's standard of living.

Meanwhile, Trevor and Teresa serve the medical needs of their neighbors back in the Korowai village. For now, Trevor says, "Korowai still are pretty low-tech and don't know how to quilt at all." Their tree-house huts aren't suited for sewing machines and quilt frames.

But at least Trevor has shown them a model of success in Nunu's village. In doing so, they may plan for a future of their own — one that includes a quilting hut and a skill that can change their village for the better.

Binding Stitch

You can help the women in Nunu's village by shopping for a quilt or other handcrafted item; for more information, write to sovereigngracemissionary@gmail.com. When ordering a quilt, please include your mailing address and the kind of quilt you want (size, pattern, colors). In an email correspondence, Trevor explains the payment plan: "Once you receive the quilt, and if you are happy, then send payment to Quilt Project, Bible Baptist Church, 3150 Sutton Blvd., Maplewood, MO 63143. If you are not happy, receive the ordered quilt as a gift." Look for Trevor's story at www .heartcrymissionary.com/trevor-johnson. Find the complete *National Geographic* article about the Korowai people at http://ngm-beta.nationalgeographic.com/archive/irian -jayas-people-of-the-trees/.

Photo on page 48 courtesy of Trevor Johnson.

Beyond Boston

On March 11, 2011, a megathrust earthquake approximately nineteen miles below the surface of the Pacific Ocean off the coast of Japan rocked the world. Scientists declared afterward that the 9.0 tremblor actually shifted the earth's axis by 10 to 15 centimeters. More noticeably, unspeakable destruction occurred in northeast Japan and could be measured on a scale much larger than centimeters. Not only the earthquake — the largest ever recorded in Japanese history — but also the subsequent tsunami wreaked enormous damage. Numbers tell the story:

15,889 dead
6,152 injured
2,601 missing
127,290 buildings collapsed
1,020,777 buildings damaged
7 meltdowns at nuclear-power plants
$235 billion (U.S. dollars) in estimated damages

But the numbers, as staggering as they are, don't tell the whole story. They don't tell about church groups from southern Japan making bus trips to the affected area to help in any way possible. They don't describe how U.S. sailors participated in rescue operations, at great risk to their own health because of nuclear leaks. And they don't tell about a group of American women who, upon hearing the news, started organizing fund-raisers and making quilts to help and encourage survivors.

The Japanese Women's Club of Boston, established just a year before the Fukushima (pronounced *foo-koo-shee-mah*) disaster, offers social opportunities and monthly lectures. Its membership welcomes like-minded, independent women who "have a desire to improve themselves and respect others."

But on March 11, 2011, their focus shifted. The group's website explains: "After the Great East Japan Earthquake, Japanese living in Boston were restless and wanted to do something. This was the beginning of Tewassa, and we started from what we could do. We want to cherish ideas born from feelings of love and support for Japan."

Tewassa is Japanese for "handmade." A more literal concept might be "played with in the hands." Japanese women took the idea literally, choosing to use their hands to offer moral support for their Fukushima counterparts. Meeting in Gray Mist Studio & Shop in Cambridge, they organized several projects.

First, they set up an interactive display at the Boston Children's Museum. Using precut quilt blocks, 124 children visiting the museum wrote messages to earthquake and tsunami victims in Japan. Afterward, volunteers stitched the blocks into a quilt and sent it to Okawa Elementary School in Miyagi Prefecture, which had been hard-hit by the quake.

Next, the Japanese Women's Club spread the word on Nantucket Island, and residents wrote messages on quilt blocks. The resulting quilt found a home at Iisaka Elementary School in Fukushima.

A third project, similar to the first two, involved the Japanese Language School of Greater Boston, where students spend Saturdays studying Japanese culture and language. In the aftermath of the earthquake, they also wrote messages and decorated quilt blocks, which were later sewn into a quilt. This project has a large red center block with a Red Sox logo signed by the team manager, along with other embroidered and signed blocks. A blog by Tewassa member Tomoko describes the quilt: "It is called Red Sox Quilt. Of course this is real Bobby Valentine's autograph. This Red Sox Quilt is our biggest quilt, and there were many encouragement words all over."

Tewassa plans to continue making quilts to show support. At this writing, the group is working with Brookline High School, in nearby Brookline, Massachusetts. Students there are making a quilt to be donated to a high school in Minamisoma, Japan. In addition, Tewassa has collected squares for a quilt to be delivered to a school in Iwate, Japan. The project goal is 144 squares.

A Japanese American blogger named Keiko invites the community to get involved in Tewassa. She says the Gray Mist Studio welcomes her group each Saturday afternoon. "No experience is necessary — just a willingness to learn," she asserts. "Many people who have never picked up a needle or operated a sewing machine before have worked on our quilts. Children have helped with the sewing. Even Boston's Consul General of Japan, Takeshi Hikihara, picked up a needle."

Keiko adds that interested persons who can't attend the regular meetings may participate by donating a 6-inch square quilt block, decorated or signed. Or they may donate fabric or other supplies such as thread, pins, beads, fabric pens, or marking pencils.

But Tewassa's ultimate goal goes beyond quilting, which it considers an opportunity to establish a connection to Japanese communities affected by disaster. Japanese American women in Boston also want their quilts to serve to educate local children about the disaster and the recovery efforts throughout northern Japan. "By working together with children, the hope is to raise the next generation with skills and knowledge to help in future situations," they declare on their website.

Tomoko, in her blog, summarizes the success of Tewassa's efforts: "A lot of people are participating in this project and thinking about those in Iwate, Miyagi, Fukushima, and Japan. A lot of heartfelt messages were put together and became big quilts."

Binding Stitch

Tewassa receives funding through the sales of handmade goods and through donations, though it is not officially a nonprofit organization. If you live in or visit the Boston area, ask about Tewassa at the Gray Mist Studio (www .graymist.com). Even if you don't speak Japanese, you're still welcome to attend its informal workdays. Keiko says, "We've had a few non-Japanese speakers join us on Saturday afternoons. Everyone in Tewassa can speak some English, so if you don't speak Japanese, that's okay!" Learn more about the group at www.tewassa.org/en. You can read about the Japanese Language School of Greater Boston at www.jlsboston.org. More information and photos can be found on Tomoko's blog (http://tomoko-photo.com/blog /quilts-for-japan-with-tewassa) and Keiko's blog (http:// japaneseamericaninboston.blogspot.com/2012/07/tewassa -handmade-with-love-in-boston.html).

SMILING WITH A QUILT

Driving into the city limits of almost any small to midsize U.S. town, you'll see a welcome sign along the road. Besides the name of the city, the sign might feature community bragging rights, such as "Home of the 2012 State Wrestling Champions" or "Watermelon Capital of the World." And if you slow down, you'll notice the emblems of the town's various service clubs, including Rotary International.

What exactly is this group? It's an organization dedicated to "Service Above Self." Rotary Clubs across the country offer four avenues of service: within the local club, within the context of members' vocations, within the community, and on an international scale.

So how can quilting fit into the picture of businesspeople's "service above self"?

You'll have to look internationally for the answer. Rotoplast, a project that receives support from many Rotary Clubs, takes place in villages around the world. Since 1993, medical volunteers and assistants travel in teams to disadvantaged areas one or more times a year. When they arrive, they set up surgeries in consenting hospitals with one goal: to repair cleft palates and cleft lips in children who wouldn't otherwise get this service.

In many developing countries, the shame of a cleft facial feature requires the child to wear a towel over his or her head when in public, said Bridget Burns, former president of the Wells (Maine) Rotary Club. Even more tragic, some children are abandoned by the roadside.

Bridget described in an online video her first experience with the Rotoplast surgeries. While in a village in Bolivia more than ten years ago, she rejoiced over the relatively simple procedure that removed the shame — for the child as well as for the family. Additionally, she noticed that each child, after surgery, was wrapped in a sterile, white plastic blanket, taken to recovery, and then sent home.

Terry Hodskins, a fellow Rotarian, heard about Bridget's experience after the medical team returned to the states. Terry considered those white plastic blankets and wondered why colorful quilts couldn't be used instead, then given to the children to take home. She remembers thinking about a quilt for each child, but Bridget objected, "You can't do that!"

"Yes, I can!" Terry recalls saying with a laugh. "I'm a Rotarian, and I'm a redhead!" She immediately contacted three quilting groups in which she held membership and

This example of a Rotoplast quilt features child-friendly fabrics and measures 48 by 64 inches. (Quilt made and photographed by the author.)

asked if they would help. All agreed. "And that," says Terry, "was the start of Wrap-A-Smile. It just kept growing and growing."

More recently, she joined an online quilting group called Sunshine Quilters, who are scattered across the United States and abroad. "From this group," she declares, "I have received quilts from every state and four foreign countries," for a total of over twenty thousand for Wrap-A-Smile.

Bridget traveled with other Rotoplast surgical mission teams since that first trip to Bolivia. She took Wrap-A-Smile quilts with her, and in a video she gushes when describing the joy of a mother who "for the first time is seeing her child without the 'broken lip,' wrapped up in the most adorable quilt, and it's clean and personal and made with love by women and men all over the United States."

She pauses and adds, "Then it's like the mother expects she's going to have to hand the quilt back, and we say, 'No, no, no. That's for you — for you and your child — to take home.' The doctors couldn't say enough about what these quilts mean, not only to the children, but also to the parents." Many homes regard their quilts as prized possessions, family treasures.

Indeed, quilts seem to speak an international language, understood by families, surgeons, and the quilt makers themselves. One stitcher, Lois Carpenter, of Spokane, Washington, enjoys creating Wrap-A-Smile quilts. Why? She says the patterns and colors are simple and fun. Also, quilters can fashion an attractive bedcover almost on a whim. For example, one morning Lois planned to reorganize her sewing room. She found a cute piece of animal fabric and a matching solid fabric. She started to toss them into a giveaway pile, but then decided to make a Wrap-A-Smile quilt. She stopped cleaning out the room and made a quilt instead!

Like Lois, quilters across the country and beyond will continue sewing for Wrap-A-Smile, because volunteer doctors will continue doing cleft palate and lip surgeries. A colorful quilt for a child recovering from surgery, Terry says, makes a world of difference. "I have to let the quilters know, it really works!" These quilts are being used and treasured, thanks to Rotary's involvement in Rotoplast surgical missions.

So the next time you take a road trip, check out the welcome sign at the towns you enter. If you see the Rotary emblem, you can offer thanks for Rotoplast's work of changing shame into smiles with surgeries and quilts in villages around the world.

Binding Stitch

For more information about Rotary International, see www .rotary.org. Bridget Burns is now deceased, but you can still watch a video of her and Terry Hodskins, as they describe Wrap-A-Smile quilts (www.wellsrotary.org/Wrap-A -Smile.cfm). A medical mission trip costs thousands of dollars, and you might consider donating to this worthy cause. Of course, the project always needs quilters. The website offers specific instructions for making a Wrap-A-Smile quilt. If you're interested in serving on a medical team with Rotoplast, see www.rotaplast.org/volunteers/medical.php#, or contact your local Rotary Club.

Golden Arches. We see them everywhere — in cities, at interstate exits, and in shopping malls — and we immediately recognize the ubiquitous fast-food giant with its burgers and fries. But behind the arches is a humanitarian organization that most people never see. If they did, they'd definitely be impressed.

Ronald McDonald House Charities (RMHC) stretches around the world and focuses on holistic, family-centered care. Its mission statement includes this assertion: "We believe when you change the life of children, you are impacting their families, their communities, and ultimately changing the world."

One arm of RMHC is its fifty-one Care Mobile units, which address critical needs of children and, as of 2014, operate in fifty-eight countries and regions of the world. Plans under way at this writing include new Care Mobile Chapters in India, Fiji, Jordan, Pakistan, and Trinidad and Tobago.

Another arm includes the money RMHC gives each year to partner organizations that help children in areas with urgent health issues. In 2014 alone it gave $8.1 million in grants. And don't forget its scholarship program: during a recent year, RMHC awarded $1.7 million in scholarships to more than two thousand college-bound high-school students.

Yet another little-known arm is the Family Rooms,

which RMHC has established in hospitals around the United States and beyond. In fact, twenty-seven new Family Rooms opened in 2013, including facilities in Australia, Mexico, Chile, and Colombia. These dedicated spaces offer parents a place to unwind and decompress with their sick child, while remaining in close contact with hospital staff.

All these behind-the-scenes offerings help countless people, though most McDonald's customers don't even realize they exist. However, one branch of RMHC has a more public presence. It may be housed in a high-rise building or a cozy bungalow. It may be part of a huge city or a small town. In any case, the sign on the building says it all: Ronald McDonald House (RMH).

Even casual hamburger customers probably know that the 337 Ronald McDonald Houses offer temporary living quarters to families of sick children. RMH's philosophy can be summed up like this: the very best medicine for a child might not be medicine at all; it might be family.

RMH believes the presence of a family helps tremendously in the child's well-being throughout a hospital stay. That's why this charity has spent millions of dollars to provide living quarters for mothers, fathers, and siblings of seriously ill children.

Take, for example, Mona Santoya and her baby girl, Genevieve, who live in Portland, Oregon. One night, Mona heard the child gasping for air. After a frantic trip to the ER, the family learned that Genevieve would need treatment at Lucile Packard Children's Hospital in Palo Alto, California.

The baby, whose heart was failing, made the 660-mile trip with her mom, while Dad and siblings stayed behind.

Mona recalls keeping vigil at her daughter's bedside in the new hospital. She says, "For nearly a week, Genevieve and I were all alone." She watched the machine keep blood pumping through the baby's system, she held her hand, and she waited.

"Luckily," she remembers, "a room opened up at the Ronald McDonald House, right next to the hospital. This meant my husband and five other children could temporarily relocate to be with us. Now we could help Genevieve get better together."

The Santoya family felt comfortable at their new digs, and they immediately bonded with other families facing similar circumstances. Mona says, "We were afforded the time, free of any other distractions, to be at the hospital to give Genevieve as many hugs, kisses, and 'I love yous' as we could." In time, she asserts, "The pieces slowly came back together, and Genevieve received her new heart and healed enough for us to return home as a family."

Thousands of similar stories fill the halls of Ronald McDonald Houses. Not only do the houses offer a place to live; they also provide home-cooked meals prepared by volunteers, along with comfortable beds for everyone in the family. And on many of those beds, family members sleep under cozy quilts.

The Northern Star Quilters' Guild of Somers, New York, is just one example of quilters who stitch bedcovers for Ronald McDonald Houses. Northern Star members, in one year alone, made fourteen big quilts and donated them to the RMH at the Maria Fareri Children's Hospital in nearby Valhalla. Caryl Castellion, president of the guild, says, "These quilts cover the queen beds in each room, bringing a family feeling to an otherwise institutional setting."

The guild also makes hundreds of smaller quilts for siblings' beds at Ronald McDonald Houses. Either way, families see the quilts, made with love and care, and they feel pampered during an otherwise stressful situation.

So when you order a burger and fries at the Golden Arches, think beyond the food. Think of scholarships, of Care Mobile units, and of Family Rooms. Think of hospitalized children whose families can stay nearby in Ronald McDonald Houses. Think of quilts that grace the beds in those houses. And be impressed.

Binding Stitch

You can help Ronald McDonald House Charities in a variety of ways. Start on a local scale by calling your nearest RMH to ask about its needs. Or check with your quilters' guild to see if members already donate. Peruse the RMHC website for more ideas (www.rmhc.org). In addition, you can see the ways Caryl Castellion's guild helps out (www .northernstarquilters.com).

QUILTS FOR PANAMA

It's less than two thousand miles from Starkville, Mississippi, to Panama. The entire flight takes only a few hours, but when the plane lands, visitors realize they've come to a dramatically different place. True, the capital city looks like a trendy urban environment of the kind featured in travel brochures, and the sun-kissed beaches attract tourists yearning for lazy days under palm trees. Also true, many retirees from the States choose to settle in and around Panama City, lured by good prices for real estate. There are countless testimonies from expats living the dream life in Panama while roaming its beautiful coastline year-round.

But the country has another side: its poverty. Dirt roads feature plenty of potholes and erratic drivers in dilapidated vehicles. The working person's diet usually consists of rice and beans, and the per-capita income is less than one-third of that in Mississippi. In spite of this — or maybe because of it — the warm, gracious Panamanians welcome visitors with a new brand of Southern hospitality.

Sylvia Jinkerson and her husband, Perry, discovered this when they took a group of Mississippi State University students to central Panama. Their group flew to the capital city, then traveled 120 kilometers by truck to El Valle, population 6,200, situated on the floor of one of the largest inhabited volcano craters in the world. There, they drove a few more kilometers to Lisa and David Carter's missionary residence. The Carters focus their efforts in El Valle as well as in a nearby indigenous Indian village.

Sylvia, Perry, and their team hadn't come for a vacation. They planned to spend their time helping the Carters in a variety of projects, such as building repairs and preschool ministry. They expected their days to be filled with sweat and sawdust, diapers and dishwater, hammers and hacksaws. But two things surprised them: cool nights and warm quilts.

After arriving, they found their sleeping quarters, set up dormitory-style for visiting mission groups, and they saw an array of brightly colored quilts covering all the twin beds. Sylvia immediately felt at home. "There are lots of ways to help people," she remembers thinking when she saw the quilts. "Little things that David and Lisa did made us feel we were important and what we did counted too. The quilts were a part of it." As she settled in for that first night, she planned to sleep well in preparation for work the next morning. "I knew I could be refreshed and ready to serve," she says, thanks to the quilts.

Those quilts originated a year earlier, with a friend in Florida. Betty Poteet, who's known Lisa Carter since childhood, says she "just wanted to do something special for her." During a conversation, she and Lisa discussed the dormitory's bunk beds, which, they decided, could use some quilts.

Betty swung into action. She enlisted the help of fellow quilters at the Concord Street Church of Christ in Orlando. These women, some as old as ninety, have an ongoing ministry, Betty declares, of making a quilt for every baby at church, for all military members in the church, and for all the elders. In addition, the group makes an auction quilt each year as a benefit for a local Christian school.

Somehow, they found time for this new project, setting a goal of a quilt for every bed in David and Lisa's dormitories. Always eager to support mission work, the quilters donated their time and skills, while other church members gave money for supplies.

Once pieced, the twenty-two tops traveled across town to the Cornerstone Quilt Shop, where Judy Dickerson used her longarm machine to quilt each one, free of charge. A few weeks later the finished quilts traveled back to the church building. That's when Betty Poteet added a label to each: "Presented to David and Lisa from the Concord Street Church of Christ quilt group." Next, the women displayed the quilts for the entire congregation to see. In the midst of the "oohs" and "aahs," Betty recalls someone's concern about shipping so much bulk overseas. But another person offered a quick solution, according to Betty: "One of the deacons came up with the idea of vacuum bags, and he shrank four suitcases of quilts into two suitcases."

Now the quilts were ready for their longest trip. To ensure their safety, Betty again appealed to her congregation, who responded with enough funds to send the head of the mission committee and one of the church elders to deliver the quilts personally. When the two men arrived in Panama with their luggage, Lisa and David received them gratefully. "We live in the mountains, and it gets cool at night," Lisa says. The quilts would be used to greet every mission team — about one a month — who came to help with preschool and children's ministry, building projects, and other church-supporting activities.

Lisa, thankful for the many hands that made and sent the bedcovers, says, "Our visitors sleep under a variety of beautiful, colorful quilts during our cool nights, and our dormitories look homey and inviting." As a bonus, the two church representatives discovered a life illustration to use when preaching. On the Sunday after they arrived, Lisa recalls, "Robin Pruitt, the elder on the trip, gave a sermon based on the idea that the church is similar to a quilt — made up of many individual pieces joined and connected by the backing of the love of Christ, which ties them all together."

The next time Sylvia and Perry Jinkerson take their college students from Mississippi State to the Panama mission, they'll overlook the poverty and potholed roads. Instead, they'll focus on meeting more warm and receptive Panamanians, as they help with the work of the church and sleep under homey quilts at night.

Binding Stitch

In Orlando, Betty Poteet quilts for several other charities and is a member of Lake County Quilters Guild (www.lakequilt guild.com) and Florida Cabin Fever Quilters (www.florida cabinfever.com). If you're interested in gathering a group of college students for short-term work in an impoverished country, you can learn more through Mississippi State University's campus minister, Perry Jinkerson (www.starkville church.org). You can find information about David and Lisa Carter's mission at their sponsoring church's site (www .wrccfamily.org/about-us/missionaries/94-david-lisa-carter). And, if you ever visit Orlando, stop by the Cornerstone Quilt Shop to meet Judy Dickerson (http://cornerstonequiltshop .sharepoint.com/Pages/default.aspx).

TEXTILE ART WITH A PURPOSE

Thirty-five million. That's how many people live with HIV and AIDS, according to the World Health Organization. Although every region of the world must face this crisis, the area known as Sub-Saharan Africa has the largest number of cases. Kenya alone reported 1.6 million people living with HIV in 2013. Sadly, the disease takes its toll on all ages, and widespread fallout includes over a million orphans in Kenya; numbers in other nearby countries are similar.

Across the globe, individuals and organizations work to prevent the spread of this deadly pandemic. A quick internet search reveals various government initiatives, medical work, educational tools, and missionary efforts — all with the goals of eradicating HIV and offering assistance to people affected by HIV/AIDS. But there's another group, perhaps surprising but no less powerful, stepping into the battle: Canadian grandmothers.

The Stephen Lewis Foundation's Grandmothers to Grandmothers Campaign is a movement of more than ten thousand people and 240 groups nationwide. These groups support African grandmothers and the children in their care by raising funds and awareness. Since its launch in 2006, the campaign has raised more than $21 million for the Stephen Lewis Foundation (SLF).

The foundation works with community-based organizations in Africa to provide care and assistance to women, orphaned children, and grandmothers. Its work began in

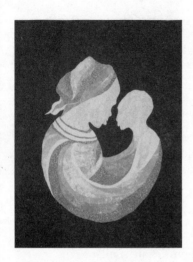

Joyce O'Connell made and donated this wall hanging, which she calls "Unconditional Love," to the Grandmothers' Textile Art Exhibit.

2003, and it has funded over eleven hundred initiatives and partnered with more than three hundred community organizations in the fifteen countries hardest hit by AIDS and HIV. In particular, SLF concerns itself with the struggle to care for the millions of children orphaned by AIDS.

Canada's grandmothers have partnered with SLF to mobilize assistance for Africa's grandmothers. One example is the Omas Siskona group in Ontario. In 2006, a few of its founding members met African women at SLF's Grandmothers Gathering at the International AIDS Conference in Toronto. The meeting, observers say, constituted "the dawn of the grandmothers' movement."

Today, Omas Siskona has more than 130 members, and it's open to any woman in Ontario's Kitchener-Waterloo area. The group meets monthly but has no membership fees. Funds for administration come from voluntary donations. Each meeting helps to increase understanding of the issues facing African grandmothers, and keynote speakers offer information and opportunities for discussion. In turn, Omas members make their own presentations to schools, community groups, and churches, educating as many as possible about the needs in Sub-Saharan Africa.

Such education garners vital financial support for the Stephen Lewis Foundation. Most donations arrive in the form of checks, cash, or credit-card payments. But another kind of donation made a big splash across Ontario in 2014–15.

That's when the Textile Art Exhibit traveled around the country and featured dozens of stunningly unique quilted wall hangings. Patterned after similar textile art shows by grandmothers in western Canada, the exhibit is entitled "Creating Futures, Threads of Hope for African Grandmothers." Its twofold goal is to acquire financial assistance and educate the public about the Grandmothers to Grandmothers Campaign. The projected goal of $50,000 is well within reach at this writing, thanks to both online and live bidding for the small quilts. Moreover, positive comments from exhibit visitors indicate the second goal has been attained multiple times already.

Ardith Chambers, who has made a number of these quilts as a member of Glacier Grannies in Courtenay, British Columbia, explains the rationale behind the grandmothers' decision to auction the quilts. Though they originally chose raffling as a fund-raiser, they discovered a problem. She recalls another group's attempt to buy a raffle license from the government. Because that group had planned to send its funds abroad, it was denied the permit. Ardith says her grandmothers group responded by nixing the raffle of one large quilt. Instead, they asked for individual wall hangings and sold them at auction. This eliminates the need for a raffle permit and allows the proceeds to be used overseas.

Even Ontario's children joined the cause. When the 2014 exhibit opened in Waterloo, 2,490 attended, including dozens of kids who stepped up to a booth to create bird or leaf figures out of fabric. Later, the figures were appliquéd and pieced into a quilt to be auctioned at the exhibit's conclusion the following year.

The adults' contributions also reflected eager involvement. One of the quilts, a 15-by-16-inch creation, featured figures of an African grandmother and child walking along a rugged path. A large container — perhaps a bucket of water — was balanced on each of their heads. Quilt maker Isobel King says the black border with hands outlined in gray represented the Stephen Lewis Foundation's support. In addition, she says, "The grandmother and grandchild are holding hands, signifying the help they must give each other in order to survive."

Another wall hanging depicted a rural African hut. Quilter Mary Ann Gilhuly says she got the inspiration from an elderly grandmother in Malawi "who was caring for four orphaned grandchildren in a hut with a mud floor and a leaky roof." Gilhuly explains that a community organization supported by the SLF repaired the woman's roof and helped her with food. If a grandmother has a livable house and a patch of land for a garden, she will sustain her family, the artist asserts. "They can go from starving to thriving."

Numerous other small quilts rounded out the traveling exhibit. Piecing, appliqué, ink drawings, beads, and other embellishments showcased the quilt makers' skills. But the wall hangings did more than that. They showed the heart of African grandmothers — women who have experienced the profound grief of losing children to AIDS coupled with the profound responsibility of caring for young grandchildren. How can they endure?

Another quilt by Mary Ann may have answered that question. Her three-paneled vertical piece, 14 by 18 inches, presented grandmothers in a variety of joyful poses. She says: "They struggle for everything, walk for water, carry food, care for their grandchildren, yet they are happy. They love to sing and dance, and I am sure that this makes their toils easier. I dedicate this piece to the grandmothers who discover joy through dancing."

Perhaps a song or a dance can give a moment of joy to African grandmothers in their daily lives. But in the long term, assistance from their communities and the Stephen Lewis Foundation will give them hope as they face the future. They'll continue to fight AIDS by caring for those closest to them. And Canadian grandmothers, thousands of miles away, will support their efforts.

Binding Stitch

The Grandmothers to Grandmothers Campaign is constantly expanding and now includes groups in Canada, Scotland, Australia, and the United States. Even if you're not a grandmother, you can participate as a "grandother." Learn more at www.grandmotherscampaign.org. Also check out the Omas Siskona (www.omas-siskonakw.org), the Glacier Grannies (www.glaciergrannies.org/textile-art/gallery), and the Stephen Lewis Foundation (www.stephenlewis foundation.org).

Photo on page 68 courtesy of Stephen Lewis Foundation.

Wrap Them in Love

Around the world, children can sleep in a bit of love and comfort, thanks to one woman's vision. In 1980, Ellen Sime and her family decided to increase their number by adopting a baby girl from Korea. Through the long months of the adoption process, she waited and wondered: Is someone holding my baby when she cries? Is she fed and taken care of properly? Has anyone hugged her?

Her new daughter arrived, but Ellen never had her questions answered. Three years later, she faced the same worries when the family again applied to adopt — this time a son. Is anyone holding and hugging him?

Years have passed, and Ellen's children have grown into adults. Yet she's never forgotten her concerns about little ones who don't feel a hug of love or comfort. Now a quilter and the owner of a fabric shop in Mt. Vernon, Washington, she recalls, "One day I was stitching a baby quilt for display in my store. I was thinking about children around the world waiting for a family and what I could do for them." In an instant she got an inspiration. "I could wrap up a child in this quilt!" she said to herself, imagining that the child would feel the love stitched into it.

From this simple idea, Ellen has established a broad network known as Wrap Them in Love. The nonprofit organization's mission is "to collect donated quilts and distribute them to children around the world, so they can be wrapped in love and comfort." Ellen points out that quilts are lovingly created and quilters leave a part of themselves in every quilt they make.

Quilts made by Wrap Them in Love volunteers find homes locally as well as around the world, and Ellen is always looking for more quilters. Fortunately, many have responded to the call.

One example is a fourth-grade class at Hinsdale Elementary School in Edgewood, Kentucky. They used permanent markers to draw pictures on fabric pieces, which were stitched into quilts by Kitty Nagy, a Wrap Them in Love supporter. The artistic quilts were hung on display at the school for parents and friends to see and then shipped to Wrap Them in Love headquarters. From there, they will scatter around the world to children in need.

Across the country, a class of sixth-graders in Presidents Elementary School in Arlington, Washington, made quilt blocks. Besides writing their names on their blocks, some students wrote an autobiographical sentence and drew self-portraits. Even the school principal made and signed a block.

A third group of quilt makers comes from the world of scouting. The members of Junior Girl Scout Troop 630 of Granite Falls, Washington, earned their textile merit badges by making and donating a quilt with signatures on white and green fabric — Girl Scout colors, of course!

In other cases, individual quilters donate to Wrap Them in Love in memory of a friend or relative. The website has a page to honor those loved ones. Ellen says, "This is not meant to be a page for sadness, but a place to remember these special people. So, in our sorrow, we mourn them, but we also honor them and remember them."

Ellen realizes interested persons may not necessarily be quilters, so she encourages them to consider sponsoring a quilt. For a financial donation — depending on the size of the quilt — Wrap Them in Love will make a bedcover and add a label indicating the quilt has been donated in the sponsor's name. Ellen suggests extending this idea for a birthday or Christmas gift. The sponsor can send a card announcing a quilt has been made in the celebrant's name.

But no matter who makes or sponsors the quilts — or why — these gifts of love must be distributed. Ellen has found a variety of ways to do this, sometimes coinciding with her own background as a mother of internationals. She tells about a woman who went to Bangkok for a visit, stuffing seven quilts into her suitcase from Wrap Them in Love. "She planned to take them to an orphanage," Ellen explains, "but at first she had a hard time finding a place to take them." After many false leads, the woman finally found a children's home run by Father Joe. "All of the children have AIDS," Ellen says, "so there's not much of a chance that they will ever be adopted. Thankfully they have each other, and they have Father Joe!" And now they have quilts as well, with a promise of more when the woman goes to Thailand again.

Another traveler took another set of quilts. Ellen's friend Sherry went to Vietnam to adopt a baby girl. Before leaving, she stopped by Ellen's shop and told her she'd take as many quilts as she could fit into one carry-on. Ellen says, "Let me tell you, I worked to stuff those quilts in that bag, and in the end I got six Wrap 'Em quilts to fit, for her to carry with her to Vietnam." Sherry delivered the quilts to the International Mission of Hope in Hanoi.

In another corner of the world, children at a Mexican orphanage also treasure their quilts from Wrap Them in

Love. Ellen says the orphanage has very little support and cannot buy luxuries. Even the children's clothing must be shared among them. Yet each child has a quilt on the bed, and the facility's matron conveys their gratitude and joy in having a possession to call their own.

The children who receive quilts from Wrap Them in Love cherish them. One touching example comes from a boy named Alexander. Adopted from Russia as an elementary student, he has learned to speak English quickly in his American home and has acclimated to the culture without major problems. After only twelve weeks in the United States, he proudly considers himself Russian American and loves school. But with all his blessings in his new home and new country, his mother says he still sleeps every night with a Wrap Them in Love quilt, which he received at the orphanage in Russia. "It is his most treasured possession," she reports.

So around the world, whether in Mexico, Russia, Vietnam, or elsewhere, children need to be wrapped in love, Ellen believes. One woman's vision can do that in a big way.

Binding Stitch

Now's the time to pull out something from your stash and make a 40-by-60-inch child's quilt for Wrap Them in Love. You can gather a group of quilting friends, or present the idea as a challenge for a crafters' group or church class. Follow sewing instructions and check out hundreds of quilt photos at www.wraptheminlove.org. Even if you don't sew, you can still help with a monetary donation.

Sunshine 4 ALL

If you ask Simon Haskins of Castle Hill, New South Wales, about acute lymphoblastic leukemia (ALL), he'll tell you it's a rare form of blood cancer that affects about three hundred Australians a year. It causes a massive overproduction of immature white blood cells, which invade the bone marrow. As a result, Simon will explain, the affected person suffers anemia, frequent and repeated infections, and excessive bleeding and bruising.

Simon may then point you to an ALL website, which lists other symptoms, such as bone pain, swollen lymph nodes, chest pain, and abdominal discomfort due to a swollen spleen or liver. Sadly, he'll say, this disease affects children from birth to age fourteen more often than people of any other age.

But Simon won't talk long about ALL, even though he was diagnosed in 2013. Instead, he prefers to talk about the cure — and the unique way he's found to push for that cure.

Simon has worked in the quilting industry for years. His mother, Jenny Haskins, is known worldwide for amazing and elegant machine-embroidered quilts. She's also the dynamo behind a line of books, patterns, and magazines. Using her renown as a starting point, Simon hopes "to raise money and awareness about blood cancers for the Leukaemia Foundation, to support those with this horrible disease. Hopefully we will one day have a cure."

He thought of an idea during the first phase of his medical treatments. He would encourage quilters and machine embroiderers to make 8-inch square quilt blocks. In turn, these blocks would be stitched into quilts and auctioned as fund-raisers. He dubbed his idea Sunshine 4 ALL: The Leukaemia Quilt Project.

His idea captured the imagination of the Australian people. Alex Perry, a leading fashion designer down under, created the center block for the first Sunshine 4 ALL quilt. From that point, hundreds of others have contributed blocks. Simon says many quilters and embroiderers have made multiples, "with some people making twenty blocks or more!"

Simon has posted guidelines for the blocks, requesting shades of orange, since that's the awareness color for leukemia. Splashes of pink or yellow can round out the palette. He also asks that each block be an 8½-inch square, unfinished, and that participants sign their blocks with a permanent archival marker. Additionally, Simon includes guidelines for crib quilts, requesting the same 8½-inch blocks, but allowing any bright color plus orange.

Even though the Sunshine project began with embroidered quilt blocks, it seems to be branching out. "This is a work in progress and nothing is set in stone," Simon writes on his website. "My hope is that this is an enjoyable, uplifting, and motivating experience." He says whole families are getting involved, and children have taken the idea outside their homes. "I already know of two day-care centres that are participating, and kids are painting blocks." He says some preschoolers' blocks display simple handprints, while others depict the sun. Simon accepts them, saying, "The options are endless." In fact, he's encouraging children of all ages to take part, because "leukaemia affects everyone and is the number-one cancer in children."

The donated blocks will be stitched into quilts and sold to raise funds for leukemia research, but Simon considers each one a gift to him personally. "This project will be a wonderful distraction for me and hopefully will motivate me on my darkest days and remind me of all the wonderful people who have donated their time and have given me the precious gift of love and support."

If you ask, he'll offer more positive news: ALL is usually curable in children, thanks to chemotherapy and radiation, along with stem-cell transplants in some cases. Rates of cure for adults are more variable, but Simon remains hopeful. He encourages quilters and embroiderers to spread the word at their local needlework shops and clubs. When that happens, he says, "Then we can really start to make a difference."

Binding Stitch

All of Simon's quotations are from his website, where you can learn more about his worthy projects at www.sun shine4all.com/launch-of-sunshine-for-all-the-leukaemia -quilt-project. You can help support Sunshine 4 ALL by buying a wristband (www.sunshine4all.com/store) or by making an orange quilt block to donate. See photos on the project's Facebook page (www.facebook.com/sunshine 4allo1). In the United States, you can learn more and donate at www.lls.org.

HAPPY ANNIVERSARY!

Ann Reeves, a quilter in Eureka, Illinois, wanted a memorable celebration for her thirtieth wedding anniversary. Nothing typical, like jewelry or a bouquet of roses. No candlelight dinner at a classy restaurant. Not even an ocean cruise. What she wanted was a plane trip — to Nicaragua.

Few couples think of Central America as a celebratory destination, but Ann had her reasons, and her husband agreed. They flew to Jinotega for a week-long working vacation at Misión Para Cristo. Their duties included painting, caring for children at hospitals and clinics, installing water filters in homes, and helping with vision and dental clinics.

The mission started in 1998 with a simple goal: to help eighteen children go to school. Today, Misión Para Cristo has enrolled twenty-seven hundred children in twenty-seven schools, all certified by the Ministry of Education. But there's more to the mission than education. The schoolchildren also receive food, medical and dental care, parasite medications, and vitamins.

Now that the organization is well established and the schools run smoothly, Misión Para Cristo's children and teachers are able to use their resources to serve the broader community. They do this primarily through the Casa Materna program.

This program, consisting of satellite centers around the country, was created by the Nicaraguan government in the 1970s. It provides medical care for women with at-risk pregnancies. Some Casa Materna locations enjoy comfortable accommodations, but not all, says Ann. She visited one that was well-furnished, although another "had only a few beds, no refrigerator, an open woodstove for cooking, and an outdoor sink that provided the washing place for everything."

But regardless of the relative comforts, any Casa Materna is better than nothing. According to Misión Para Cristo: "Most of these women live in remote areas of Nicaragua with limited or no health care. They may travel from an hour to several days to reach the closest Casa Materna, where they stay until they deliver their baby, in order to be near a health center or hospital." What's more, these women usually come alone, leaving older children behind

Nicaraguan women at Casa Materna show off new quilts made by American volunteers.

to tend to the house and chores. The expectant mothers' desire to deliver healthy babies overrides other considerations. That's why they seek out Casa Materna.

Janese Davis has lived at Misión Para Cristo since 2010 and works primarily with Casa Materna. When mothers-to-be enter any one of the six Casa Maternas near Jinotega, they receive a special gift from the mission: a baby bag with a Bible, diapers, a blanket, baby wash and lotion, wipes, a onesie, and socks. Many of these items come originally from the Gerber company, which has registered Misión Para Cristo as an official charity.

Along with the gift bags, the mission teaches basic health care for women, their babies, and their families. This, says Janese, may be the key to helping young mothers. When groups from the States come to the mission, they add personal care to this education. Janese notes that they "make a day-long trip to visit one of the Casa Maternas and spend their day serving those women." The personal contact, coupled with health-care classes, can touch lives like nothing else.

Another way to touch lives is through quilts. Casa Materna residents receive homemade baby quilts — as long as the supply lasts. The 38-by-44-inch quilts come from volunteers around the United States and are warehoused by members of the Judsonia (Arkansas) Church of Christ. Karen Chalenberg, church secretary, says her congregation sends twenty or more adults and teens each year, along with over a hundred baby quilts, to Misión Para Cristo. However, if the mission runs out of quilts, Janese says they have a backup plan: receiving blankets, which some churches send along with their quilt donations.

A few years ago, volunteers made a surprising discovery at Casa Materna. Women enjoy not only receiving the baby quilts; they also enjoy making them. Janese remembers the reason for that discovery. Some pregnant women arrive weeks or even months before their due dates. She says, "These women have nothing to do but sit and wait for their baby to be born." On one occasion, while distributing quilts to the mothers-to-be, Janese and her coworkers got an idea: "We already did some crafts with them, so we thought we would have them cut their own squares for a quilt." Out came scissors and fabric, and the Casa Materna residents got to work. They cut out 6-inch squares, made their own quilts, and felt a sense of accomplishment in the process.

Since then, individuals, women's groups, and even quilt shops around the country have been cutting squares and packaging them in sets of forty-two, along with a backing, to be shipped with the next mission group to Jinotega. The motto of Misión Para Cristo, since 1998, has been "Just One More," says Ann Reeves. So she'll piece just a few more baby quilts for Casa Materna mothers, to go along with the donated squares. "It has been a joy for me to make these little quilts," she says, and she'll send her creations with a group traveling from Judsonia.

Or she may decide to take them herself — on her next anniversary trip to Nicaragua.

Binding Stitch

To learn more about Misión Para Cristo, see www.mision paracristo.com. To donate baby quilts or quilt squares to

Casa Materna, contact the Judsonia church (www.judsonia churchofchrist.org). Or ask your friends, neighbors, or co-workers if they know of another humanitarian group that travels to impoverished countries. You may be able to coordinate a quilting project through them.

Photo on page 80 courtesy of Rebeka Molina and Casa Materna Cihuatlampa.

SPREADING THE COMFORT, KEEPING THE FAITH

QUILTING AT THE FARMHOUSE

Every Tuesday for more than twenty-five years, a handful of women have pulled into the driveway of the Bailey farmhouse near Byron, Michigan. They recognize the stately Queen Anne by its four porches and tall windows. In summer, baskets of potted petunias swing from the overhangs, and in winter, snow drifts across the steps.

From the side porch, the women enter the country kitchen, complete with floor-to-ceiling cabinets along one wall and a back stairway on the other. They walk past the kitchen table and through the doorway, with its Victorian-style rosette corner blocks, into the dining room. From there they can see the front room through a double-wide door sporting more rosette blocks. A bedroom converted into a den sits to the left, and the nearby front stairway leads up to four more bedrooms. If the women glance through the double-hung windows, they can see rolling farmlands growing corn and soybeans or — depending on the season — blanketed in snow.

But they're not here to admire the architecture or the view. They're here to make quilts.

Their hostess, Evelyn Bailey, welcomes them, and after a few minutes of friendly chatter, they get to work. Someone picks up a rotary cutter and a couple of yards of fabric. Someone else sorts 5-inch squares into complementary colors. Another person sits at the sewing machine in the den, and a couple of others join Evelyn at the dining table.

That's where a twin-size quilt top is layered with batting and backing. And that's where the women use strands of yarn to tie the layers together. Afterward, someone else cuts binding, which will be machine-sewed onto the new quilt. On a good Tuesday morning, when all runs smoothly, these women might piece, layer, tie, and bind a couple of double, twin, or baby quilts.

The group started unintentionally — and not as quilters. "Five of us from church went to a missionary meeting in Flint," Evelyn recalls. "The missionary showed craft items that someone had made for her and her people. She said even those little things can be used as gifts to show love to others."

From that presentation Evelyn got an idea. "On the way home I told the other women that the Lord keeps telling me we need to do something." All agreed, brainstorming ways to serve with their skills. Within days of that meeting, she says, "we started making a few craft items, but we didn't know what to do with them." After all, doilies and doll booties might bring a smile at Christmas or raise a little money at a bazaar, but could they really make a difference in someone's life?

During another brainstorming session, one of the group members came up with the idea of quilts. No, not the prizewinners at the fair, and not the ones garnering "oohs" and "aahs" at a show. Many of these women didn't have skills for that kind of work, but their friend Dorothy Yeagle could teach them the basics. That led to their decision to make functional quilts — ones that would be used and appreciated.

Ideas flew like needles at a bee, and they eventually

agreed to donate serviceable quilts to the Carriage Town homeless center in Flint, to Youth Haven in Rives Junction, and to the crisis pregnancy centers in Flint and in Owasso. They chose each of these charities because they wanted to touch and transform lives.

First, the homeless shelter offers meals and beds to the neediest in the community, and those beds always require sturdy, washable quilts.

Second, Youth Haven helps disadvantaged youth ages seven through thirteen by providing learning experiences in a fun and safe Christian environment — all free of charge. All attendees, who stay for a week-long camping experience, have economic, emotional, family, or social problems. Many come from single-parent or foster homes and are usually recommended by social services or school counsel-

ors. When Evelyn and her group began donating to Youth Haven, the quilts were used on the children's beds. More recently, according to the organization's secretary, quilts are given to children as Christmas gifts.

The quilters' third major recipient provides hope and help to young women facing difficult choices. The Flint Crisis Pregnancy Center accepts quilts and gives them to mothers and babies. The organization also works with fathers and encourages two-parent teams when possible. Evelyn says, "If the parents complete a Bible study at

Doris Boillat poses in the farmhouse kitchen with one of the quilts made by the group who meets in this home.

the center, they are given a chest filled with a baby layette" and other gifts, including maternity clothes and baby furniture.

By contrast, the Pregnancy Resource Center in Owasso has different plans for donated quilts. As in the case of Youth Haven, the use of quilts at this charity has changed over the years. Katrina Voorhies, client services director, says some quilts are sold at the center's boutique, where the proceeds buy baby supplies for new mothers. "Women make these things and donate them out of the goodness of their hearts," Katrina says. "These women do make a difference in someone's life."

Besides these organizations, Evelyn's group donates quilts to individuals. "We send quilts to overseas missionaries," she says. "And if neighbors have a fire and lose their home, we'll give the family a few quilts." After a pause, she concludes, "We give them to people who need them."

Muriel Hibbard, Evelyn Bailey, Cheryl Green, Tina Petty, and Doris Boillat work on layering and tying a charity quilt in the farmhouse.

Recently, eighty-two-year-old Evelyn has been forced to curtail her quilting efforts. But the work continues. "Right now I have fifty quilt tops upstairs," she says. "They're ready to be made into quilts. But I've got arthritis in my hands and can't do much myself."

That doesn't stop the group, though. "I'll still call the ladies over here and they can work," she declares.

They'll come to the Queen Anne farmhouse, where many of them have cut, pressed, and sewed weekly for almost three decades. And they'll continue to touch lives, because, says longtime participant Doris Boillat, "A warm and beautiful quilt is a comfort to anyone, especially when sewn with love."

Binding Stitch

You can make quilts or donate other items to a homeless shelter in your area. Contact one today and ask how you can help. Youth Haven has camps only in Michigan and Arizona (www.youthhaven.org/faq#sthash.JmFsGIDz.dpuf), but almost every state has a similar organization. Use your search engine to find one nearby, and contact it to see how you can help. Likewise, crisis pregnancy centers are found in most major cities, and all of them appreciate donations. Contact the one near you to learn of its needs.

Photos on pages 88 and 89 courtesy of Doris Boillat.

CHURCH QUILTS

Instead of starting a major quilt project with a book of patterns, Jacklyn Schwarting Powers started with a camera.

She and granddaughter Anna donned hiking boots for a trip into the Sierra Nevada Mountains near Clovis, California, one bright day in late September. When they reached a particular slope, they stopped to rest and snap photos. As the breeze ruffled their hair and rustled leaves in nearby trees, they breathed the clean mountain air and took even more photos, especially directed eastward.

They knew this site had already been purchased by Jacklyn's church, Divine Mercy Catholic Church. Once funds were raised, the parish would build here, with its front doors, according to Father Craig Plunket, facing east.

A quilt design inspired by the location began to take shape in Jacklyn's creative mind. It would eventually become a reality and serve to remind her parish of its blessings in the natural world. But that quilt was only one of many Jacklyn would make as she served her community.

Back in 2008, Jacklyn and friend Jan Clagg discussed the possibility of showering homebound persons with small gifts. Besides lotion, cologne, and gloves, Jacklyn considered quilts, and she approached her informal group, which met at Quilters' Paradise, a local shop. When she presented the idea to the eighteen or so regular participants, they immediately agreed to help. "Today," she says, "our group donates more than one hundred quilts every year to homebound seniors."

Word has spread, and Jacklyn says women outside the group often "donate part of their stash to us. Our stash has grown from half a dozen plastic storage bins to an 8-by-10-foot room." Amazed by the generosity of strangers, she adds, "We also have 'angels' who donate cash to buy batting and any other supplies we need." Although most members of Jacklyn's group work on cutting, piecing, and quilting at the shop, others take projects home and then bring back the finished quilts the following month. "All of these people are equally important to the ongoing survival of our project," she says.

To emphasize their importance, Jacklyn organizes a reception each December at the quilt shop. Here, all the quilts from that calendar year are displayed, and the public is invited for a viewing.

Jacklyn enjoys being a part of this ongoing endeavor, but she also has a few projects of her own. One of them she calls the Crucifix Quilt. While her church is being built on the mountain slope, the parish meets in a high school's multipurpose room. Jacklyn thought a large wall hanging would make the location feel more like a church and less like a gym.

So she designed a Christ figure and a cross, adding background colors reminiscent of those she remembered from a time when she'd lived in the Middle East. Next, she found a local student who drew the Christ figure, and Jacklyn pieced the cross in wood-grain fabrics. She then pieced the background in Log Cabin blocks with a light sky, rusty hills, and brown dirt.

Two aspects of this quilt set it apart from any other. First, the Christ figure is "attached, but not totally," Jacklyn explains. "I had the drawing enlarged to just over 5 feet tall. My granddaughter, AnnaMarie Rieffel, traced the enlargement onto muslin. She used Sharpies to add dimension and detail. I then made a light sandwich [assembled the top, batting, and backing], stitched some of the details for emphasis, and cut it out." To make the figure as realistic as possible, Jacklyn attached it by hand to the cross at the head, the hands, and the feet, "so he appears to be hanging."

A second unique aspect of this project involved the quilting process. After binding, Jacklyn decided to include her parish family in the final details. "I brought it to Mass for three Sundays, so any parishioner could add red or white stitches," she says. "Many parishioners stitched away. Parents helped their children add stitches. Adult children helped our seniors. Both men and women added their prayerful stitches." Naturally, the stitches aren't tiny or uniform, but they represent the love, faith, and unity of that parish.

Now the quilt is hanging in the school's multipurpose room, "in front of floor-to-ceiling windows," Jacklyn describes. "At the eight-thirty Mass the sun streams through, and we have a 'stained-glass' window."

Another of Jacklyn's major quilt projects also benefited the parish, but in a different way. The Sierra Sunrise Quilt, a 100-inch square masterpiece, was sold at auction to raise money for the building fund. And it all started with Jacklyn's camera.

Like the design of the Crucifix Quilt, the Sierra Sunrise pattern didn't come from a book. Jacklyn, after viewing her photos taken on the parish's building site, decided on two hundred half Log Cabin blocks, 5 by 10 inches each. She chose colors to match the pictures, using her knowledge of color combinations from thirty years as an elementary-school art teacher. For the next six months, Jacklyn worked on the quilt, adding clouds, trees, fields, grasses, rocks, and even a fence. Every element included authentic features, like embroidered barbed wire strung between fence posts and tiny flowers and weeds at the base of each post.

Throughout the months she spent on this quilt, she kept a journal of her progress and of the spiritual insight she gained. She says the writings of King David in the Old Testament often gave her encouragement. Frequently she thought of Psalm 121:1, which says, "I will lift up mine eyes unto the hills, from whence cometh my help." She also got encouragement from her fellow parishioners — "people who have become like family." She says, "I wanted to share with these wonderful people. They have welcomed me with open arms and hearts. I only hope the quilts have given them some of the joy they have given me."

The Sierra Sunrise Quilt was one of several items auctioned at a Diamonds and Denim fund-raiser, named in recognition of both businesspeople and ranchers in the parish. Jacklyn says the money she spent on supplies and fabric for the quilt was recovered many times over, thanks to generous bidders, and thousands of dollars in total proceeds went into the church's building fund.

And the quilt itself? The winning bidder donated it back to Father Craig, so it will be part of the church family for years to come.

Binding Stitch

If you're interested in making a quilt for your house of worship, plan first! Consider the available space, color choices, aesthetics, and the wishes of staff and members of the congregation. If you don't belong to a faith group, you can still make a quilt or wall hanging for a meeting room. Think about groups you attend. Ham radio club? Grange hall? Garden club? Surely almost any location can be brightened with an appropriate quilt on the wall. Like Jacklyn, you might want to keep a journal of progress as you work on this quilt — especially if it's intricate and time-consuming. You can include "dos" and "don'ts" for future projects as well as photos, swatches of fabric, and names of people who helped you. As a bonus, you can give a copy of your journal to the person who receives your quilt, as Jacklyn did to Father Craig. Meanwhile, check out the quilt shop in Clovis, California (www.quilters-paradise.com), and learn about the charity work headquartered there.

Unlikely Quilters

Quilters — some of them unlikely volunteers — seem to come out of the woodwork:

- Employees in a Chicago office bring portable sewing machines and dedicate Friday lunch breaks to quilting.
- Dartmouth College students join senior adults to make quilts in Hanover, New Hampshire.
- Men and women in Nampa, Idaho, brave a blizzard to gather in a church basement for a quilting marathon.
- A group in Sheboygan, Wisconsin, enlists young children to decorate blocks with fabric crayons, while their parents piece quilts.

These examples and dozens of others illustrate the lure of quilt making, which can link generations and skill levels, all for a good cause. The examples above are part of the Quilt Campaign of Lutheran World Relief, which encourages groups to make hundreds of quilts every year for underprivileged people around the globe.

Lutheran World Relief (LWR), an accredited charity with the Better Business Bureau, cares for health and emergency needs in parts of South America, Africa, and Asia. Through its agricultural strategies, HIV/AIDS prevention, malaria relief, and clean-water projects, LWR is a leading organization in the fight against world poverty. Quilts play a part in this work.

Across America, Lutherans and others stitch simple quilts, 60 by 80 inches, for children and adults in third-world countries. These quilts may be used in a variety of ways in addition to their traditional purpose as bedcovers. For example, a quilt tied around a mother's back can become a baby carrier; it can serve as a sack for transporting vegetables to market, then be spread on the ground to display and sell the goods; it can be a sunshade or a shawl, depending on the weather. Most important, the website says, a quilt can be "a constant reminder that someone, far away, cares a lot."

In a typical year, almost half a million donated quilts travel first to an LWR warehouse in Maryland or Minnesota, where they're sorted and boxed for overseas shipping. Meanwhile, staff members consult with partner organizations in various countries to determine their needs. Quilts are then shipped to Afghanistan, Nigeria, the Philippines, India, and more than a dozen other locations. Throughout the process, LWR communicates with partners overseas to ensure the quilts will reach the intended recipients.

Hundreds of Lutheran groups and individuals donate quilt after quilt, year after year, to LWR. Even people who normally don't see themselves as quilters get caught up in the excitement of doing something worthwhile.

One example, mentioned briefly above, involves a group started by Wendy Bertram. While on an extended vacation in Michigan's Keweenaw Peninsula in 2005, she visited a church with an active quilting ministry. She knew

In churches across the United States, quilts are made, dedicated, and donated to Lutheran World Relief.

nothing of the art and craft of quilting, but she learned the basic skills that summer. When she returned to her own congregation, St. Peter Lutheran in Sheboygan, Wisconsin, she recalls, "I announced on a Sunday morning that I would like to start a quilting group for Lutheran World Relief, since I'd learned how to make quilts that summer."

The response made her head spin. "I was amazed that so many women were interested," she says. "Years earlier, some members had started a quilting ministry, but it fizzled due to members losing interest, aging, or moving out of the area." However, this time proved different. Wendy and her enthusiastic followers dusted off the church's sewing machines, found fabric still in storage, and got to work.

This group certainly hasn't fizzled. They continue to meet the second and fourth Tuesdays of each month, except in the summer. The church's women's ministry bought two additional sewing machines and other supplies, like batting, thread, and scissors. Even more astounding, Wendy says, is the regular donation of fabric. "It never ceases to amaze me, all the fabric that arrives in the sewing room. Where does it come from? I don't know. It just arrives!" Obviously, the whole congregation has an interest in this ongoing project.

To encourage that interest, the quilters invite everyone to an occasional workday. Wendy describes one church-wide quilting session: "We set up seven or eight sewing machines, tables to cut squares, tables to lay out the squares, tables to put quilts together, and tables to tie the quilts." Sunday school teachers prepared 8½-by-11-inch pictures, which children as young as four years old colored with fabric crayons. Next, adults transferred the artwork onto plain fabric squares by ironing. Others then laid out the blocks alternately with solid-colored squares, and the sewers pieced them into quilt tops.

Those children's art quilts were finished and given to a sister congregation in Apopa, El Salvador, and to the church's own pastor, Diane Loberger, during her cancer treatments. But the majority of St. Peter's quilts find a home overseas through LWR. Exactly where they end up, Wendy doesn't know. "We do not track our quilts. We assume that they go where they are supposed to go, and we pray that they are a blessing to those who receive them."

So the Tuesday group keeps churning out quilts — with pleasure. "We laugh, we tell jokes, we sing, we pray and just enjoy each other's company," says Wendy. "Some of us have been friends for forty-plus years, some are new members who just like to quilt, and some are not even members of our church."

But all — from experienced quilters to unlikely newcomers — work in the hopes of improving others' lives. LWR describes these quilts as "Tied in faith. Sent in hope. Wrapped in love." That's true of quilts made in a Chicago office building, at a New Hampshire college, and even in a small church in Sheboygan, Wisconsin.

Binding Stitch

To see the LWR Quilt Plaza in Baltimore, go to www.lwr .org/donate/quiltplaza. If you're interested in making quilts for LWR, check out the Q&A page (www.lwr.org/get involved/FAQ) and the scrapbook of churches involved in quilting (www.lwr.org/scrapbook).

Photo on page 98 courtesy of Beautiful Savior Lutheran Church, Spokane, WA.

Jelly Rolls and Envelopes?

At first glance, jelly rolls and envelopes seem unrelated to each other and certainly unrelated to quilts, but in the long run there's a definite connection. And it all starts with a couple of friends in Davison, Michigan.

Both members of St. John's Catholic Church, quilters Anne Winiarski and Nancy Kramer meet with their Blanket Ministry twice a month. Together they spend hours making blankets and quilts for Phinisee Outreach for Women, providing housing for persons recently released from jail; for Heartbeats, supporting very young mothers and pregnant teens; and for Catholic Charities. In fact, when Anne and Nancy's friend Sue Feller asked Father Andrew Czajkowski about starting a sewing group, he agreed — as long as their focus remained on Catholic Charities, which provides a variety of services to people in need.

Catholic Charities in the United States (CCUSA), in many Americans' minds, evokes images of soup kitchens and homeless shelters. It does those things, but it also advocates for issues such as immigration and refugee assistance, workforce training, and support for disabled and marginalized citizens. More prominently, CCUSA works on behalf of poverty-stricken persons. Its website says, "Together we are dedicated to creating a life of opportunity and self-sufficiency for each of the forty-six million of our brothers and sisters who live in poverty."

Topping the list of needs among these "brothers and

sisters" is housing. Although Catholic Charities helps find affordable, permanent homes for people across the country, fully one-third of its housing budget goes toward transitional living arrangements. Examples include St. Joseph's Home in Denver. Expressly for homeless veterans, St. Joseph's provides short-term residents with education, rehabilitation, and hope, while arranging long-term housing elsewhere. Across the country, St. Francis Recovery Center in Auburn, Maine, offers a residential rehabilitation program, which terminates when the former addict moves into his or her own house. And in central Michigan, CCUSA's transitional housing serves men, women, and children as they prepare to settle into rental units.

Nancy and Anne's Blanket Ministry, a group of about ten, makes quilts for this transitional housing program as well as for other area shelters. They've branched out from Catholic Charities but have remained faithful to their promise to the priest.

Because of all these "branches," Nancy stresses the importance of producing many quilts as quickly as possible, so her group developed a jelly-roll process. Most quilters have heard of the jelly roll, a packet of dozens of precut 45-inch strips of fabric, all the same width, stacked and rolled into a coil that resembles the colorful pastry. Fabric shops usually offer jelly rolls in a 2½-inch width, but Nancy's group prefers 6 inches, because "6-inch strips go together much quicker," she says.

Before each meeting, Nancy precuts matching fabrics. Other volunteers sew those strips with long sides together, making quilt tops approximately 60 by 80 inches. Once the group gathers, they layer the quilt tops with batting and backing using the envelope method. Nancy explains: "We lay out the batting first, then the quilt top right side up, and then the backing right side down. We pin only along the outside edge." This process seems contrary to normal layering, but after three sides are sewn, the "envelope" can be turned right side out and the fourth side stitched closed. The quilt is now layered, with no need to add binding. Next comes tying, and the job is finished.

"We're more concerned with quantity," says Nancy. "That's why we can provide as many quilts as we do." They may not be works of art, she admits, but "they're useable." During the Blanket Ministry's first eighteen months, volunteers made 132 comforters and quilts with this method, and by the end of 2014 they'd made 250.

When the quilters need thread and other supplies, they naturally call on church members. Nancy says, "Our group has put announcements in our church bulletin several times, asking for donations of fabrics, thread, batting, sheets for backings, and blankets and mattress pads for batting." Always, church members respond generously — and sometimes surprisingly. "We have received a large variety of items, including several quilt tops," Nancy points out. "The better-quality quilt tops we quilt and bind in the traditional manner. Father Andy has allowed our group to hang these quilts behind the welcome desk." She says the St. John's Catholic Church Family Center has classrooms, meeting rooms, a gym, a walking track, and a physical therapy center. Parish members pass the welcome desk on their way to other activities. As a result, she notes, "We have sold several quilts in a short period of time."

The Blanket Ministry's philosophy focuses on the

individual recipient. "The quilts are meant to be given to the person who receives them first," Anne says. "They shouldn't be passed along." That's why the women at St. John's feel compelled to work fast. When residents of Catholic Charities and other shelters move on to permanent locations, they take the quilts with them. So Blanket Ministry must stitch and layer more quilts to replace them.

Anne and Nancy say they joined the group for pleasure and friendship. As Anne observes, "This is a nice way to meet people. It's easygoing. Nobody's critiquing your work." But they've discovered another, more important aspect of Blanket Ministry. They've discovered the premise that has governed Catholic Charities for years. Giving to help others is pleasure in itself. Sewing jelly-roll strips, stitching together a "quilt envelope," or delivering finished bedcovers to the homeless shelter — all provide joy to the giver and to the recipient.

Anne tells about her little grandson, who asked, "Why are you making blankets to give away, Grandma?" She then explained the Blanket Ministry to him, delighted that he showed an interest. "Maybe," she says, "one day he'll see the importance of volunteering too."

Binding Stitch

For general information about Catholic Charities, look in your phone book or go to www.catholiccharitiesusa.org. You can learn specifically about homeless assistance in central Michigan at www.womenshelters.org/det/phinisee

-outreach-shelter-for-women or at the local Catholic Charities site (www.catholiccharitiesflint.org). Elsewhere, use your computer search engine or the phone book to discover nearby homeless assistance. In every case, these shelters need basic supplies, like paper products and kitchen goods, and they need quilts — sturdy, utility quilts for everyday use.

COMFORT AT
BEGINNING
AND END

TINY STITCHES

At age eighty-three Friederike Faust keeps her fingers nimble by sewing and knitting. "I learned to do all that when I was in school," she says. "But maybe they don't teach that in school anymore."

Perhaps not, but Friederike (whose nickname, Rike, is pronounced "Ricky") learned her lessons well, and she now uses them in a grand way in rural Georgia. She volunteers with Tiny Stitches, a program that assists poverty-ridden mothers. Tiny Stitches offers basic items for newborns whose families are not able to provide for them. In addition, it supplies bibs and tote bags to home-visiting services as well as complete burial ensembles for infants who've passed away.

Tiny Stitches volunteers, who range in age from twelve to ninety-seven, work through hospitals and clinics in the ten counties around Atlanta. They collect donated fabric and yarn along with money for other supplies. In turn, they distribute these materials at workshops, held in various towns in the area. Stitchers and knitters then produce finished items, such as sleepers, crib quilts, tote bags, caps, blankets, booties, and sweaters. Tiny Stitches holds an annual social function, so that all the scattered volunteers can meet and receive recognition for their work.

A few years ago, Rike learned about Tiny Stitches from a friend. "I was at a fabric store, and a woman I'd known for forty-seven years was talking to someone else about this charity. She then turned to me and asked if I had time to help." Rike pauses for a laugh. "I said, 'No way! I don't want to do anything where I just sit around.'"

The friend didn't give up. For months afterward, she persisted with invitations, and finally Rike agreed to attend one — and only one — Tiny Stitches meeting. That proved to be her undoing. "When I saw the stuff they were making," she recalls, "I was hooked." Immediately she volunteered to knit baby caps and booties.

In a well-worn ledger book, she keeps track of the number of caps she's knitted over the years: 442. The list of footwear is even more astounding: 3,000 pairs. "They're not real booties," she admits, explaining that her creations cover more of the leg than traditional infant footwear does. "I made up my own pattern, because babies normally kick off the regular booties. I made these into a sock pattern. The ladies at Tiny Stitches went wild when they first saw them, because little babies won't kick them off." With a pause, she runs the numbers. "I can knit one sock in two hours, so a pair takes four hours. That means I've been knitting these socks for twelve thousand hours."

Then, in 2004, she started quilting. She decided to ramp up her work at Tiny Stitches by sewing a simple, three-layer bedcover for every needy newborn. "They're not fancy quilts," she says. "They're thirty-six by forty-five inches. The back is one piece of flannel, the batting is Fiberfill, and the front is some kind of matching color." She's made 942 of these quilts.

And she's not about to slow down. She says the quilts aren't showy and don't take long to make, but when a new mother has absolutely nothing for her baby, a warm, colorful bedcover of any kind is a blessing. It's also a way to give mother and baby a connection to someone who cares.

Rike plans to work as long as she's able, knitting and sewing in her free time. Her greatest wish is to convince others to join her cause. She takes her knitting wherever she goes, and she explains Tiny Stitches to anyone who will listen. Meanwhile, she and her group continue to serve disadvantaged babies in and around Atlanta. Obviously, Friederike Faust learned more in school than just knitting and sewing. She must've learned compassion as well.

Binding Stitch

Contact your local hospital and ask about opportunities to volunteer your handiwork as Rike does. If you live in the Atlanta area, you can learn more about Tiny Stitches, a not-for-profit charity, at www.tinystitches.org/about_us or at P.O. Box 254, Suwanee, GA 30024.

QUILTED MEMORIES

Louisiana native Jack Tolar, nicknamed Pete, served in the air force and army national guard, then in law enforcement, retiring from the Catahoula Parish Sheriff's Department after thirty-five years. His credentials are impressive by anyone's standards: Chief Criminal Deputy, Sheriff's Mounted Patrol Rescue Team, Narcotics Task Force member, emergency medical technician. On top of all that, he held a black belt in jujitsu. But Paige Peoples thinks of him simply as Dad.

A few days after he died, she stood in the bedroom her parents had shared for fifty years. Her mother, nearby, sorted through his clothes, arranging them in neat piles on the bed. Paige watched and felt a new wave of grief wash over her. "In my mind, I didn't want to part with any of his things. All I could think about was wrapping myself up in them, to feel like I was with him again."

In that moment, Paige conceived a way to accomplish exactly that. "The thought came to me of a quilt I could give to Mom, and we could all enjoy it and think of him. I told her of my idea, but first I had to find someone to make it."

Enter Barrett Beasley. Barrett, Paige's longtime friend, is a partner in the law firm of Salem-Beasley, LLC. She practices products liability and pharmaceutical litigation before state and federal courts, arbitration panels, and appellate courts. The intensity of her job demands some kind of release, and after her career took off, Barrett searched for an activity to help cope with the stress.

"About ten years ago," she recalls, "I inherited my mother-in-law's ancient Singer." Barrett couldn't sew at the time, so when a visiting friend saw the machine, she poked fun, asking Barrett if that piece of furniture was just for looks.

Spurred on by the challenge, Barrett decided to give herself a year to learn sewing. She enrolled in classes and soon created several garments. "Then I took a quilting class, and I was hooked. It was like a disease with me — I couldn't stop making quilts," she recalls with a smile. She'd found her de-stressor.

Since her discovery of quilting, Barrett comes home after long days in court and turns to her library of patterns, a stash of fabric, and the sewing machine. When a quilt is finished, she finds her greatest pleasure in the giving. "With rare exception I give all my quilts away," she says. "Sometimes to loved ones, sometimes to near strangers. It just feels like the right thing to do — put warmth and comfort out in the world."

One of her favorite recipients is Court Appointed Special Advocates (CASA). This nonprofit organization, with chapters across the country, works on behalf of children who've been moved out of abuse or neglect

Barrett Beasley donated this strikingly bold quilt to CASA in 2014.

and into foster care. Barrett, who volunteers as an advocate, makes a bold geometric quilt each year for CASA's fund-raising auction.

A dramatic example of Barrett's generosity occurred in connection with one of these fund-raisers. Barrett's donated quilt went to the highest bidder, while the second-highest left empty-handed. But an unrelated occurrence produced a much greater sorrow for this losing bidder. Barrett explains, "Shortly after the event, her sister died in a drowning accident. It was so tragic. I turned around and made a quilt to give to her."

Barrett's willingness to do this for a stranger prompted her friend Paige to request a quilt from her father's clothes. She and her mother chose a variety of garments in "Daddy's colors" — mostly blues and khakis. Since Mr. Tolar had loved Cabela's pants, Paige requested that one of the company labels be stitched onto the quilt.

Barrett agreed and received the clothing on a Friday. The project intrigued her, and she began working that evening. "First," she says, "I started cutting everything apart to see what I had." Her collection included pants and flannel shirts, shorts and jeans. Then she looked through quilting books to find a pattern, finally settling on a modern one featuring a variety of rectangles.

Always thinking of the grieving family, she stayed true to her mission. "I didn't want to supplement with any other fabric. Even the binding is from one shirt." The result is a bold, masculine quilt, complete with a leather Cabela's tag stitched onto the back. After piecing, Barrett sent the top, batting, and backing to a trusted longarm quilter, and in a matter of weeks the gift was ready.

Paige accepted the quilt in October but decided to wait until Christmas to present it to her mother and the family. By this time, Paige recalls, "Mom had completely forgotten about it. When she opened the box on Christmas morning I was on pins and needles wondering how she would react." Her mother fingered the quilt but didn't realize its significance for a moment. "Then she gasped," Paige says, "as if she was seeing Dad. She immediately knew it was his clothing. She and the rest of us burst into tears."

But, for the first time since Pete Tolar's passing, the tears weren't from sorrow. Paige believes they were "happy tears, because I think we were all glad we had this trivial part of his life." Memories of the impressive military man, deputy, EMT, and black belt — also known as Paige's dad — will live on, she says, "made new by Barrett's gift of sewing."

Binding Stitch

Making a quilt to remember a deceased loved one can be a warm and rewarding gesture, especially if that person's own clothing is involved. You might consider stitching such a gift for a friend or family member. Be sure, however, to use compatible fabrics. Barrett's quilt will hold together well, because all of Mr. Tolar's clothing was similarly rugged and coarse. For other projects, Barrett uses the quilter's standard: 100 percent cotton. You can learn more about her favorite charity at CASA's website (www.casaforchildren.org).

Photo on page 112 courtesy of Barrett Beasley.

LONG-TERM QUILTS

"We feel like it is the best community project we've ever done." That's how Sharon Clark describes the involvement of Missouri River Quilt Guild (MRQG) with aging veterans in Columbia, Missouri. And, she admits, it all started when she made a whopping promise that the guild couldn't fulfill.

Since 2008, Sharon has helped out at Harry S. Truman Memorial Veterans Hospital, which serves forty-four counties in Missouri and one across the border in Illinois. "I volunteer there once a week, in the long-term care unit," she says. "The head nurse knew I was a quilter, and she asked if maybe our guild would be interested in making quilts for the beds in this unit." The nurse thought quilts would give a homey look to the twin beds and offer comfort to the older vets.

Sharon, a quilter for about six years at the time, liked the idea. "Sure, we can do it!" she recalls was her enthusiastic response.

She knew MRQG's history of community service. Through the years this small guild had chosen a variety of charities to receive its donations. The Christmas Stocking Project serves as a great example. One year, guild members made dozens of stockings and donated them to the Food Bank for Central and Northeast Missouri. In turn, the recipient sold them during a radio fund-raiser. Every donor contributing $100 received a stocking, and the Food Bank's proceeds totaled an impressive $6,800. Because of careful buying, this charity stretched $1 into $13 worth of food, which gave the donation a buying power of $88,400.

MRQG's stockings helped others as well. The Samaritan Center, an interfaith social-services agency, received several Christmas stockings from the guild and then sold them to a generous donor for $2,000. Amazingly, that donor returned the stockings to Samaritan for families in need during the holidays.

Even more stockings, donated by the guild to a food pantry known as Serve, Inc., saw double duty as well. Serve, Inc., used its stockings to hold personal-care items and donated them yet again — to Girls Town in Calwood Township.

Besides all these stockings, Missouri River members one year had made quilts for Honor Flight participants. That's why Sharon felt certain her quilting friends would happily produce a few twin bedcovers for the veterans.

These quilts were donated to the veterans' hospital in Columbia, Missouri.

But when the nurse asked for forty quilts, a stunned Sharon managed to mutter a positive-sounding response. At her next guild meeting she got the same reaction. Forty? "It was a small guild, and we only committed to making ten quilts."

Only ten. Now what? After a moment of panic, Sharon picked up the phone. By the time she'd contacted five other nearby guilds, she had a firm commitment for forty quilts. Many more poured in within the following months. "Eventually we had one hundred seventy twin quilts," she says with pride.

Thanks to this huge response, Sharon had more than enough to give a quilt to each veteran in the long-term unit. "I was the lucky one, because I got to hand them out," she says. On Veteran's Day, guild representatives held a small ceremony at the hospital, allowing each long-term patient to choose his or her own quilt.

She recalls one vet, who always wore a John Deere cap and sweatshirt. When Sharon sorted through the quilts at that ceremony and found one with a center panel of a Deere tractor, he immediately requested it. From that moment, he kept the quilt with him at all times, Sharon says. During the day, it draped across the back of his wheelchair; at night it covered his bed. This elderly veteran and farmer stayed close to his tractor throughout his final days.

After the first forty quilts were given out, Sharon and the staff found storage for the others. In the years that followed, they gave them to all new patients entering the unit. Finally — a full four years after the initial request — Sharon says they had only two quilts left: one with blocks of purple and lavender and one with a camouflage pattern containing deer and other wildlife.

Two patients checked in on the same day, and Sharon took the two quilts into one man's room. She remembers, "At first he couldn't decide. Purple or camo? 'They're both so beautiful,' he said. He eventually chose the purple." Sharon had worried that the purple's more feminine look wouldn't appeal to most men. But now she sighed with relief. When she took the last quilt to the other new patient, he grinned. He'd been a hunter all his life and loved his new camo bedcover. "It worked out so well!" Sharon says.

Missouri River Quilt Guild has moved on to other charity work, but its best-ever community project lives on as veterans enjoy their quilts, which keep them warm at night and brighten their hospital unit by day. As Sharon notes, "The quilts seemed to have the most impact and last the longest."

Binding Stitch

Your local veterans' hospital always needs volunteers. You might consider being a patient escort, a driver, a "cheer chat" companion, or a coffee-cart operator. Call the hospital or find these opportunities online. If you're thinking of making quilts for veteran patients, contact the hospital to determine the need. You'll also want to find interested groups willing to donate funds and supplies. Sharon says the approximate cost of one quilt is $150, not counting labor. She appreciates donations from quilters as well as from local nonquilting groups, including the VFW, the Ladies Auxiliary, the Navy League, and the Forty and Eight Society of Columbia.

Photo on page 116 courtesy of Missouri River Quilt Guild.

Facing the End

Nobody wants to talk about it. It makes us squeamish. Sure, we know we'll all go through it — someday. But that's a long time in the future, right? We'll deal with it later.

Even in our conversations we skirt the issue. When we meet the life insurance representative, we say, "If something happens" — as if we're not quite sure what that *something* might be. We employ euphemisms like "passing away" to make it sound more palatable. We just don't like to face it.

But one group has faced death countless times and can encourage others to do the same with peace and comfort — and the help of a quilt.

The website Ask.com defines "hospice" as a philosophy of care that involves "the palliation of a terminally ill or seriously ill patient's pain and symptoms, and attending to their emotional and spiritual needs." Though some type of hospice care has existed for centuries, its modern form developed in the 1950s, thanks to a registered nurse in Great Britain. Dame Cicely Saunders, when caring for a dying Polish refugee, confirmed her resolve to treat all terminally ill patients with compassion. She did this "to help address their fears and concerns as well as palliative comfort for physical symptoms." That philosophy governs today's hospice programs.

Hospice Home Care in Searcy, Arkansas, has applied the philosophy countless times. Its motto is: "Adding life to days, when days can no longer be added to life." In a newspaper statement, the Searcy office explains, "There are universal questions about life and death and the meaning of each." That's why its nurses, chaplains, and volunteers address those questions while seeing to the patients' physical comfort during their final illness.

Quilts can be a part of this picture. Jan Jones, RN, is a quilter with a studio in her home in Spokane, Washington. "I took the idea of comfort quilts to Horizon when I started working there," she explains, referring to her six-year stint at Horizon Hospice of Spokane. Once the administration accepted her idea, she says her quilting group at church started working. They produced a variety of quilts to suit many personality types and continue to do so, but they don't do preorders.

Instead, the hospice nurse gets acquainted with the patient and family and chooses an appropriate quilt from the stack of donations. While Jan worked there, she served as liaison between the visiting nurse and the ill person. "There is a protocol before we go to a home," she says. "I would go and meet with a nurse in charge of the patient. We would go in [to the patient] and just make a little bit of a ceremony, telling them we appreciate their life and all the gifts they've brought to the family and community." That's when the nurses present the gift. "We want to bless you with a quilt made by our group," Jan recalls saying to each family.

Lori Bradeen, volunteer coordinator with Horizon Hospice, knows the recipients appreciate the quilt gifts. Although she doesn't usually attend the gifting ceremonies, she notices the quilts during her visits to the homes. "I have seen well-used quilts that we have given them," she says.

Some patients handle their quilts daily; others want theirs to be preserved, like fine china or the family's heirloom linens.

Often the patient and family are deeply moved by this special gift. On one occasion, Jan remembers seeing a frail, elderly patient repeatedly running her hands across her new bedcover. In a whisper, a loved one said she used to be an award-winning quilter.

When possible, if the quilting group hears of such a patient, they extend their volunteer efforts in a more intimate way. Linda Shelby, RN, former nursing consultant for the Arkansas office mentioned earlier, says, "Quilting is wonderful! Sometimes a volunteer goes regularly to the home and takes a quilt project she's working on. She sits and sews and visits with the hospice patient." Not only does this give a meaningful hour to the patient; it also gives the caregivers a break, says Linda. "It really means a lot to the patient's family."

After the person's death, the quilts still serve a purpose, depending on the family's desires. Volunteers with Hospice House, also in Spokane, make quilts that cover the deceased as he or she is transported out of the house. One observer stated, "The beautifully patterned quilts are a comfort to those who escort the bodies. No sterile hospital sheets, just a lovingly made quilt."

In other cases, says Jan, they want it buried with the loved one. But more often, they keep the quilt, displaying it at the memorial service. In the months afterward they pass it from one relative to another, so that each household can treasure the memory. Some families drape the quilt over an empty chair for holiday gatherings and reunions.

No matter how the quilts are used, the volunteers find joy in making them. Quilter Karen Franks, a member of Jan's group, says she gets real pleasure in the creative process. "We have a lot of donated fabric as well as quilt blocks that people have started but never finished," she says. "I really enjoy taking what someone has started and trying to make something new out of it." She recalls a particular unfinished project she took over. "I did one that was really bright — all different stripes. The gentleman who took it said it reminded him of Joseph's coat of many colors." Of course, Karen was thrilled that her quilt "spoke to the person in need," even though she had no idea who would receive her creation when she'd made it.

While planning their quilts, members of Karen and Jan's group enjoy this level of creativity. Making quilts for unknown recipients frees them to try new patterns and techniques. Karen says, "We just all look through books to see what we would like to learn. We want to have a challenge for ourselves, plus something we would be proud to give to someone."

When this someone receives a quilt, he or she knows another person has lovingly made it. Recipients also know a deeper truth: they are facing a final battle with illness, and now is the time to talk about fears and uncertainties. Now is the time to quit the euphemisms, to quit skirting the issue. Receiving the quilt signifies facing the truth. Nurse Jan Jones, who's not afraid to discuss this sensitive topic, says, "Here you're dealing with the dying process. It's when the people opt to say 'no more treatments' — that's when they get the quilt."

Binding Stitch

You could donate your unfinished projects to a quilting group that sews for hospice, or you can make a quilt to donate. Cities across the United States and Canada, along with many other parts of the world, have some form of hospice care. Use the internet or phone book to discover a hospice program in your community. Make a call and ask if they use quilts in their end-of-life work.

Finding Your Niche

The Medical Center in Vancouver, Washington, like any other hospital, needs volunteers to handle everyday duties: greeting patients and guests, giving directions, delivering flowers, performing general clerical jobs.

The hospital also uses volunteers in specific areas, like its cancer unit. Duties include offering beverages and a compassionate ear to patients receiving chemotherapy; assisting patients who come for mammograms or other procedures; and helping staff at special events, like the American Cancer Society's Relay for Life. Last on the list: offering practical support to patients and their families by making quilts.

This is where Venita Aldrich found her niche. After her mother passed away from the ravages of cancer, she decided to give back to the community in a way that would benefit others with life-threatening illnesses. Venita had already taken training to become a hospice volunteer. But she soon discovered she wasn't suited to that work. As she puts it, "I could not give back in like manner."

After more consideration, she thought of the Cancer Injection Unit of PeaceHealth Southwest Medical Center. Venita says, "I chose this unit, hoping to help the people who have to sit in the chairs or lie in beds and have injections when it gets chilly." Of course, the hospital offers a generic blanket for each chemo patient, but a personalized quilt seems to communicate more care — especially to those who may be in short supply of care. "I asked the coordinator to provide these quilts to people who didn't seem to have a lot of support from family and friends," Venita adds. "I hoped to give a little comfort and joy to those patients."

For the first eight months, Venita worked alone on this project. But the responsibility grew, and she realized she needed help. She put a notice in the Country Manor fabric shop and got three willing helpers. "We were fortunate," Venita remembers, "that Country Manor wanted to have community charity activity." Now, a few years later, she has eight or nine at every meeting. As each person joined, the group recognized a common bond: all had been touched by cancer. One had lost a brother to the disease; another had a parent in remission. A few of the group members themselves had suffered with breast cancer.

Most of the quilts Venita and her group make are created from donated fabric and scraps from other projects. They're not too fancy, and they're not large — for a reason. "We make the quilts a certain size, to drape around shoulders," she explains, yet not interfere with a wheelchair's moving parts or footrests. Each is a rectangle 40 to 45 inches wide and 50 to 55 inches long. Venita hopes that recipients feel the love immediately, when they wrap themselves and see the label, "Because We Care." Venita recalls a particular incident. "One woman was shocked when we told her it was hers to keep, and she settled into chemo like she had a new best friend."

Hospital social worker Anne Cowan-Cleveland has a similar attitude toward quilts donated to the cancer unit. She knows the importance of matching quilts to the right patients, so she tries to discover something about them. What

One of many quilts donated to the Cancer Injection Unit, featuring cheerful, bright colors.

is their favorite color palette? Are they into sports or other hobbies? Once she asks a few discreet questions, she brings out two or three quilts that seem to fit the personality. "I make it fun," says Anne, who often drapes the quilt around her own shoulders and models it. As soon as she sees "the eyes light up and a certain look on a person's face," she knows she's chosen the right quilt.

Next, she says, the patients often express surprise that someone would make such beautiful quilts for strangers. Anne notes, "Usually, they will study the quilt, looking carefully at every block." Many patients wrap themselves in their quilts during treatments; others fold them carefully across their laps.

Chaplain Mary Katherine Lookingbill, also of Peace-Health, agrees that quilts provide untold comfort — even quilts given to patients facing end-of-life issues. She says, "If a family consents, we provide [the patient] with a quilt, the size of a single hospital bed, that was created just for this time and place. The quilt represents the love and prayers of those who made it, even though the family will never meet them."

She believes quilts add "color and comfort" to an otherwise sterile hospital environment. In fact, she says, when a staff member brings a quilt into the room, the patient and family often exclaim that its color or pattern is absolutely perfect for that person. Chaplain Mary Katherine has reported those responses to the quilters on numerous occasions, adding, "You are blessed to be a blessing to others."

But the blessing doesn't stop there. Once the patient has died, the family is invited to take the quilt home. The chaplain observes, "Leaving the hospital without one's loved one is one of the loneliest walks there is, and many, many times I've watched spouses or daughters or sons leave clutching the quilt that was on the bed of their loved one."

Certainly the patients and family members benefit from the quilts, but what about the staff? Chaplain Mary Katherine says the caregivers love these donations too. When nothing else can be done for a patient, "The quilts provide us something to do. For our caregivers, being able to either give or see these outward and visible signs of God's love is comforting for them also."

When asked about starting a similar quilt-giving project elsewhere, Anne Cowan-Cleveland says almost any hospital would welcome it. "We definitely appreciate our quilters. This is not a fun time for our patients, so having anything that brightens their day is a good thing." She likens the comfort of a quilt to the comfort of Mom's chicken soup.

Quilter Venita Aldrich concurs, advising interested persons to consider exactly how they can help and then contact their nearby hospital. She says she initially approached the cancer center with a list of what she expected to accomplish. The coordinator liked her ideas and accepted her help. Then Venita got to work to fulfill her goals.

That's good advice — especially from someone who,

through trial and error, finally found her niche. "Keep poking around, then do what you can, where you can," she says.

Binding Stitch

Chaplain Mary Katherine says she sees five hundred deaths a year and that means they "never have enough quilts!" Likewise, the cancer infusion unit admits new patients on a regular basis, and quilts are always appreciated there. If you live in the Pacific Northwest, consider making a simple quilt for either of these units of PeaceHealth (www.peace health.org/southwest/Pages/default.aspx). If you live elsewhere, do what Venita did: contact your local hospital to learn of its needs. Also, get to know nearby quilt shops and discover which ones have community charity projects. You might find your niche that way!

Photo on page 126 courtesy of Venita Aldrich.

JACK'S DAY

Jack Hughes was a little fighter. Born on May 8, 2010, he weighed only 1 pound, 3 ounces, after less than twenty-four weeks in the womb. But he fought to breathe. He fought against the NICU wires and other attachments covering his tiny body. He fought renal failure. He even fought a pulmonary hemorrhage. But two days later, his strength ran out. He lost that final battle.

After Jack died, his parents left the hospital carrying only a clear plastic bag with a few items: Jack's hand- and footprints, a baby hat, a preemie outfit, a few small stuffed animals, a pamphlet about grief, and a handmade blanket. "These items soon became our most precious possessions," recalls his mother, Emily, "because they were the only things we had that our son had ever touched." In addition, she says, a neonatal nurse had taken photos of the preemie in his incubator. Those were the only baby pictures Jack's parents had.

Even in her grief, Emily thought of others. Before a year had passed, she and her mother came up with an idea that would benefit countless families in southeastern Michigan facing a similar loss. Baby Jack's first birthday would have occurred on Mother's Day in 2011, so they dubbed it Jack's Day. The Hughes family would celebrate by donating Memory Boxes to the hospital where he'd died. When deciding what to put into the boxes, Emily says, they thought about things that someone who had lost a child would like.

"Each box," Emily explains, "contains items that are meant to bring comfort to the grieving family." When possible, the box is given by the hospital to the family and its items used during the baby's short life. Emily lists examples of contents: a small teddy bear, hat and booties, a picture frame or small album, a journal, a disposable camera, and a blanket or quilt.

This last donation is extremely important. Emily says, "Sometimes we give two blankets or quilts, so the family can bury the baby in one and take one home." In a quiet voice that speaks from experience, she adds, "Sometimes parents sleep with those blankets, because it's the last thing their baby touched."

Quilts for Jack's Day boxes are understandably small. For a full-term infant, a quilt should be around 36 inches square, but for a very small preemie like Jack, Emily suggests nothing larger than 12 inches. Members of Craftsy, an online crafting group, make quilts for Jack's Day. One participant, Melissa Smith, says in Craftsy's blog, "Since they are for tiny babies, they are small quilts, sometimes no bigger than fat quarters." She's referring to a quarter-yard measurement of fabric popular among quilters. But no matter how small, she believes all babies deserve their own quilt.

Quilt enthusiasts may see an immediate benefit of making microquilts. Melissa explains: "It's not only a good cause, but a good chance to try out new techniques and blocks on a small scale."

Like all items in Jack's Day boxes, each tiny quilt is a unique creation. In fact, Emily says, "Handmade things really make a difference." She welcomes quilts in pink and blue as well as those in yellows, greens, and other gender-neutral shades. "We try to have boxes available for boys and girls and babies we don't know the sex of," she says.

Once yearly, Emily and her friends gather to prepare Memory Boxes for nearby hospitals. As volunteers sort donated items and decorate the boxes, they talk about their own struggles with sorrow and loss. Through this activity, they feel a sense of joy in spite of grief, for they are sharing the common goal of allowing other parents to take home precious memories of their baby. The group averages about fifty boxes a year.

Jack's Day is part of a larger nonprofit known as Metro Detroit Share. This volunteer support group helps parents who have experienced loss through miscarriage, stillbirth, or early infant death. Each October, the group sponsors a Detroit Share Walk for Remembrance and Hope to raise funds and awareness.

Jack's Day shares those goals, though Emily believes the ultimate aim is helping parents themselves, especially those "who may not have a strong support system to go home to." She hopes such parents in Detroit and outlying hospitals will find comfort in the Memory Boxes. Each time she distributes the boxes to hospitals, she sees grateful smiles. Of a recent delivery, she says, "People were impressed, and hospitals were thankful."

Surely that little fighter would be pleased.

Binding Stitch

Emily is happy to receive donations for Jack's Day boxes, which will be distributed in Dearborn, Trenton, Taylor,

Garden City, Grosse Point, Wyandotte, and Detroit. Visit her at http://jacksday.webs.com/aboutus.htm, or contact her at emilyhughes88@yahoo.com. If you live in the Detroit area, you can learn more about the Metro support group at www.metrodetroitsharegroup.com, or offer to help through Craftsy (www.craftsy.com/blog/2013/10/quilting -for-charity). Emily is interested in branching out and welcomes suggestions for additional hospitals that might want Memory Boxes. However, she encourages readers to consider starting their own program in their community. She suggests calling the hospital and asking for a chaplain or bereavement coordinator.

SCHOLARLY
WORKERS

ARKANSAS PINS

They call themselves PINS, and they spend almost every Tuesday together on the campus of Harding University in Searcy, Arkansas. Liz Howell, director of the university's alumni relations, says PINS is "a dynamic group of talented women."

Debbie Howard works at the Harding History House, where PINS meets. Her assessment of the group's six to eight participants echoes Liz's: "They are delightful women, so devoted and hardworking."

PINS — People Interested in Service — has only one focus. Its members do piecing and hand quilting to raise money for needs-based scholarships to Harding, a Christian university. Harding's website says it is "committed to the tradition of the liberal arts and sciences," including nursing, pharmacy, psychology, and various fields of business. At last count, its enrollment reached almost seven thousand students from all fifty states and fifty-two other countries.

Many of those students need extra money for college, especially for a private university. So PINS helps out. Liz says, "This group has raised more than $26,000 for scholarships in nine years" — a lot of money from a stack of quilts.

Quilters at PINS work year-round, but the flurry of activity occurs in the fall. Member Sue Justus explains that during September and October PINS takes bids on the quilts they've made in the previous twelve months. "We start with our price and go up from there," she says. "We do advertisements, and the quilts are displayed at Homecoming." Because of the class reunions and other activities, hundreds of people arrive on campus that week and see the quilts. Feeling school-spirited and generous, visitors buy a quilt or two and help a student.

Scholarship recipients face certain requirements. They must have a financial need, and they must present three letters of recommendation to the scholarship committee. The amounts of money awarded vary, depending on the students' financial situations. In addition, recipients must agree to serve the Harding community through twenty hours of work each year. Such jobs might include manual labor, like hauling tables to and from Homecoming activities and Family Weekend events. Or they might simply be fun, like dressing as superheroes and entertaining children at special breakfasts. Perhaps they're a mix of labor and fun, such as assembling gift bags to sell for additional scholarship funds.

Here's where PINS has the opportunity to interact with students. Most PINS members are the age of the freshmen's grandparents, and both generations embrace that role. Harriet Raley, a longtime participant, says the quilters enjoy getting to know the beneficiaries. "We take them on while they're students," she says. "We mentor them." In this way, PINS members help encourage the scholars and hold them accountable for academic as well as community service responsibilities.

The initial meeting between PINS and new scholarship recipients occurs each spring. The alumni office holds a scholarship banquet, allowing the older women to establish a relationship with their special students, who speak at the event and offer their thanks.

Like most of the members of PINS, Harriet grew up with needlework as a way of life. "I did cross-stitch and needlepoint first," she says. "But I got interested in quilting through a sweet lady named Classie. Mother gave her our old clothes, and she'd use them to make quilts and other things." When Harriet graduated from high school, Classie gave her a package of scraps — but not just *any* scraps. "She'd cut a piece out of every piece of clothing we'd given her over the years. I made a quilt out of those scraps for my mother." Since then, Harriet has continued quilting, and she appreciates the intangible, sentimental value. "Recently I finished two T-shirt quilts for my grandsons. These boys carry on our heritage with these quilts."

Likewise, Irene Crouch's skill has a long history. As a founding member of PINS, she says she started quilting fifty years ago, but she "let it go for a while." Then she met quilter Charlotte Pigg, now deceased. "We were just getting together and quilting, and Charlotte got us into Women for Harding," whose main purpose involves raising funds for scholarships. From there, PINS emerged, as like-minded women discovered the value of their hand-quilted masterpieces.

But they don't quilt exclusively for Harding. They also stay busy with their own quilts. "We've all got projects going at home," Irene says. "After we quilt three for PINS, we do one for ourselves." Just like at an old-fashioned bee, every member in turn brings her layered quilt to the meeting room, and group members sit around the frame to finish it.

But their most important work is still the handmade full- or queen-size quilts they donate to the university. This "group of talented women" has found the perfect way to use their skills to benefit students in need.

Binding Stitch

If you live near a college or university, start a PINS group of your own. Call the admissions office to learn about scholarship needs and then gather friends to help. You can donate scholarship money in memory or in honor of someone, or you can designate that the recipient be a certain major (like fiber arts or design) or from a certain area (like a disadvantaged county in your state). Be creative, make your quilt, publicize it, and raise money for your school! Check out Harding University's scholarship offerings at www.harding.edu, or contact Liz Howell at lhowell@harding.edu.

OLD MEETS NEW

Hungarian American Mary Gasperik might shake her head in amazement at modern technology. Born in 1888, she couldn't have imagined how computers would streamline and transform the world. And she certainly wouldn't have guessed that an amazing union would take place between those newfangled computers and her beloved quilts, all pieced before 1950. But if she were alive today, she would probably embrace that union.

The Quilt Alliance understands the juxtaposition of old and new. This international group focuses on saving and cherishing America's quilting heritage using up-to-the-minute technology.

For example, the Quilt Treasures program, the Alliance's joint venture with the Michigan State University Museum and MATRIX: Center for Digital Humanities and Social Sciences, features web portraits that document the lives and work of leaders in the quilt revival of the 1960s and 1970s. And Quilters' S.O.S.–Save Our Stories presents a downloadable guidebook to individuals wishing to preserve quilt stories and photos.

So what exactly does the Quilt Alliance do? Its official statement indicates it "brings together a vital, active network of individuals and organizations nationwide." This massive network includes quilters, guilds, historians, folklorists, archivists, quilt shops, museums, and universities, all of which "celebrate and preserve the art and history contained in quilts captured by quilt makers."

Thanks to today's technology, the Quilt Alliance office in North Carolina is linked with MSU and with the American Folklife Center at the Library of Congress in Washington, D.C. In addition, the Alliance and its partners comprise a virtual worldwide community that shares information about quilt collections, research projects, and quilt exhibitions. The Quilt Index, also a partnership project between the MSU Museum, MATRIX, and the Quilt Alliance, offers digital images and documentation in the largest online database of quilts in the world.

It's enough to make your head spin. But don't get lost in the technology and miss the heart of Quilt Alliance: the quilts and their creators. Take Mary Gasperik, mentioned earlier. She emigrated from rural Transylvania to the United States with her sister when they were teens. At age eighteen she married fellow Hungarian Stephen Gasperik and subsequently had three children. After attending the 1933 Century of Progress Exposition, where she learned about quilting, she used her extensive needleworking skills to produce breathtaking works of art. Her quilts combined American tradition with Hungarian folk images to create unique designs. Between 1933 and 1967 she made more than a hundred full-size quilts along with miniatures and other small works.

Years later, Karen Finn and Susan Salser organized an exhibit of this remarkable woman's quilts, and by the early 2000s Salser had photographed and documented Gasperik's entire collection and contributed these records to the Quilt Index. The result, says the Quilt Index, "is not only the most complete photographic record of one woman's quilts, but also an invaluable resource of period photographs, newspaper accounts, and quilt-making ephemera."

Mary Gasperik's story beautifully illustrates the efforts of the Alliance and its partners to document and preserve quilt makers' work. The Quilt Index provides mountains of information and photographs of her quilts as well as thousands of others. On the index, people can find documentation and photos from private and museum collections, bibliographies related to quilting, lesson plans, and quilters' journals. There's even a Quilt Index To Go — an app for mobile devices — offering information about a different quilt each day. Proceeds from app purchases help sustain the Quilt Index.

Because of the internet, documentation can be accomplished twenty-four hours a day, but some of the best opportunities occur at major quilt shows and exhibitions. For example, early in 2014 the Alliance set up shop at the Modern Quilt Guild's first QuiltCon, in Austin, Texas. Later that year, its staff and board members conducted the Not Fade Away Conference in Virginia and the Quilters Take Manhattan fund-raiser, and they hosted a booth at the Houston International Quilt Festival. In every venue, Alliance representatives made presentations and collected interviews. These interviews, recorded digitally, become part of the Alliance's archives and can be accessed through the Quilt Alliance YouTube channel, blog, and website.

Amy Milne, executive director of the Quilt Alliance, posts the daily offering for the Quilt Index and Alliance blogs. She tries to find quilts that have historical significance as well as a current tie-in. "I look at websites like History.com and try to correlate an event with a quilt," she explains. "On [Gothic novelist] Ann Rice's birthday, I thought it would be funny if there was a vampire quilt somewhere." Sure enough, after a bit of searching on the Quilt Index, she found a quilt made by a supposed vampire in the late seventeenth century. That's the kind of thing that makes the blogs appealing to a broad spectrum of followers.

Amy says another appeal to today's quilters is the documentary project, Go Tell It at the Quilt Show! Whenever she and other Alliance representatives attend quilting events and shows, they set up a "studio" consisting of lights, a blank-wall backdrop for hanging a quilt, a microphone, and a camera. Individuals get three minutes of airtime to document their quilts. Similarly, the Alliance's Go Tell It at the Museum! coordinates with museum education and curatorial staff to create quilt videos at their own locations.

Of course, all this takes money. The Quilt Alliance generates funds through its annual membership drive. Amy says, "For us, membership is a big piece of our operational support." She compares a year's dues to one trip to the quilt shop. "It's not that much money, and we

Quilt Alliance Advisory Council member Merikay Waldvogel of Knoxville, Tennessee, presents her quilt to the Alliance's videographer at a quilt show.

wouldn't think twice about spending it when shopping," she says with a laugh. "But it makes a huge difference to us at the Alliance." Benefits? A monthly newsletter and reduced entry fees for the annual contest and other Alliance events. Also, because Quilt Alliance is a nonprofit, memberships are tax deductible.

The annual quilt contest and auction serve as another kind of fund-raiser. Quilt entries must be 16-inch squares and consist of top, batting, and backing. Other than those simple rules, the only requirement is that the quilts attempt to feature the Quilt Alliance's suggested theme for that year — in 2015 it was "Animals We Love." When finished, the entries become property of the Alliance; they are displayed at various events and then sold at a benefit auction.

For over twenty years, the Quilt Alliance has worked tirelessly to promote, preserve, and share the heritage of quilting. Its future looks bright, because more quilts and more quilt stories will surface. And people will continue to care about quilts. Amy notes, "The Quilt Alliance has built on that tradition, uniting people interested in quilts from inside and outside the quilt world."

Technology has made this uniting possible — old and new quilts, quilters and their stories. Mary Gasperik and others a hundred years ago couldn't have imagined web-based videos, downloadable tutorials, or online repositories. But one thing has remained the same, though the methods differ. As Amy says, "Quilts have always brought people together."

Binding Stitch

Examples of the historical documentation supporting Mary Gasperik's quilts can be seen on the Quilt Index (www .quiltindex.org/gallery.php?kid=48-7D-1). For more information about the Quilt Alliance, go to www.alliancefor americanquilts.org. You can join or make a donation to the Quilt Alliance (www.allianceforamericanquilts.org/support /donate.php) or donate to the Quilt Index (www.quiltindex .org/donate.php).

Photo on page 141 courtesy of the Quilt Alliance.

THREE GREEK LETTERS

At the entrance to the Family Fare grocery store in Cheboygan, Michigan, an octogenarian sits near a table. Behind her an 80-by-92-inch Maple Leaf quilt hangs on a display frame, its vibrant fall colors practically begging shoppers to buy a raffle ticket in hopes of winning. The woman, Donna Watkins, tirelessly answers questions. Yes, she made the quilt. Yes, she's been quilting almost thirty years. Yes, the raffle's proceeds will help a good cause.

What cause?

Delta Kappa Gamma.

What's that?

The three Greek letters represent an international society that promotes the professional and personal growth of women educators. The goals of Delta Kappa Gamma (DKG) include honoring teachers of distinction, supporting legislation and other activities that promote the interests of education, and endowing scholarships for women pursuing degrees in education. In addition, DKG serves as a clearinghouse for information on current economic, social, political, and educational issues.

In seventeen countries DKG has established a presence, and it currently sponsors two broad-interest projects. The first, SEE (Supporting Early-Career Educators), aims to help novice teachers establish themselves and become comfortable in their field. DKG bemoans the fact that thousands of young teachers leave the profession after only one year and even more leave after the second year.

In an attempt to stop the mass exodus, SEE assigns volunteer mentors to the novices. Mentors make phone calls and visits, help with lesson plans and classroom management issues, and offer advice on parent-teacher relationships.

The SEE program has enjoyed significant success, and Delta Kappa Gamma's website presents proof. Of first-year teachers assigned a mentor in the school year 2007–2008, only 8 percent left the profession the following year. But of the new teachers *not* assigned a mentor, 16 percent left a year later, and a whopping 23 percent left within two years. Such numbers clearly show the value of a mentor. DKG adds with justifiable pride, "We truly can make a difference with our support."

Delta Kappa Gamma's second major project focuses on only one part of the world. The Schools for Africa program benefits five million children by increasing access to education in eleven of the continent's poorest countries. To accomplish this lofty goal, Schools for Africa builds and rehabilitates hundreds of school facilities, trains thousands of teachers, and provides school supplies. The program also helps with practical needs that most Americans don't even consider: ensuring that children have safe drinking water and separate restrooms for boys and girls. As a result, schools can be a haven for learning — especially for poverty-stricken girls and orphans.

Besides mentoring new teachers and supporting African schools, Delta Kappa Gamma oversees the distribution of scholarships. Thousands of dollars are awarded to worthy recipients around the world — women who plan to study education on the master's or doctorate level. As many as thirty DKG members receive major scholarships each year, and the society claims it has given out more than $4 million since the international scholarship program began in 1940.

Such big numbers tend to boggle the mind, but on a local level it's simpler. That's where Donna Watkins enters the picture. After graduating from Central Michigan University in 1947, she taught elementary grades in Saginaw and later in Pellston, Michigan. She spent her entire professional life as a teacher, joining DKG in 1981. Now retired, she focuses on raising money for scholarships.

Referring to the Gamma Eta chapter of DKG, she says, "Each year we give a $500 scholarship to a girl entering the education field at the college of her choice. If she maintains good grades and stays in the education field, when she's a senior, we give her a second $500."

Although it's not a huge scholarship, Donna says, "They really appreciate the money. In their senior year, as student teachers they can really use it." Donna's chapter earns over $1,000 a year on the quilt raffle, which maintains the scholarship fund.

In 1986 Donna took a quilting class through Michigan State University's Extension Study program, and later she began making quilts for DKG's scholarships. Now it's an annual tradition for her: stitching the quilt and selling tickets at Family Fare. "It's our way of helping young women establish a career in education," she says.

Binding Stitch

Learn more about Delta Kappa Gamma at www.dkg.org and its African project at www.schoolsforafrica.com. DKG focuses on education, and you can join its efforts with a quilt raffle or another type of donation. Or you might want to consider a variety of other scholarship opportunities. Talk to nearby colleges and universities, but don't stop there. With enough research, you can find a scholarship tailored to your own interests or passions. Consider a culinary or art institute, beauty college, auto mechanic training center, or skilled nursing school. In every case, you'll find an eager administrator who'll guide you in establishing or maintaining a scholarship.

LITTLE QUILTS

Sometimes little things can make the biggest difference.

The National Quilting Association (NQA), head-quartered in Columbus, Ohio, holds an annual show and fund-raiser, and the proceeds from its Little Quilt Auction provide approximately $10,000 in grants across the United States. The NQA praises the generosity of both contributors and buyers of these Little Quilts, making the auction an eagerly anticipated tradition at the annual NQA show.

So what exactly is a Little Quilt? One form is a miniature of a larger quilt. These tiny creations look like scaled-down versions of full-size quilts. They're pieced in practically any pattern — Dresden Plate, Grandmother's Flower Garden, Churn Dash, for example — but each piece might be smaller than half an inch wide. Such a quilt requires patience, graph paper, and a good dose of geometry to achieve the correct proportions. But the results will dazzle the eye and confound the imagination.

Or a Little Quilt might be a doll's bedcover. After all, dolls get chilly at night, and they don't ask for the intricate piecework or appliqué that usually characterizes quilt miniatures. Instead, they need serviceable covers, which can be draped around Dolly's head like a bridal veil, tied over her shoulders like a superhero cape, or in some households wrapped around a kitten or puppy to keep Dolly company in her bed. These quilts are often made of bright, simple patterns with kid-friendly prints. They might be tied or quilted by hand or machine.

A third category of Little Quilts is wall hangings. As the name implies, these hang as works of art in entryways, bedrooms, living rooms, and dens. Their colors and patterns should resonate for viewers across the room, and their designs can be as wild or conservative as the quilt maker desires.

A Little Quilt in any category must be no more than 28 inches on its longest side, and it must be signed or permanently labeled with the names of the quilt and quilt maker along with the date of donation. Every year, NQA has high hopes for this fund-raiser. "Your contribution of a quilt or two," says the website, "helps to make a colorful display and gives those attending many choices for bidding."

Throughout the NQA's annual show, Little Quilts are offered at a silent auction. Even more compelling, a small selection of them earns the honor of a place at one evening's live auction. The quilt receiving the highest bid garners respect and recognition for its creator.

Best of all, the proceeds make possible the grants given to individuals and groups whose goals are consistent with NQA's. Grant recipients must aim to "promote the art, craft, and legacy of quilt making, encouraging high standards through education, preservation, and philanthropic endeavors." Grant applicants must be involved in some aspect of community education and outreach through quilting. The NQA awards about five grants per year, in amounts ranging from $100 to $3,000.

One worthy recipient in 2014 was the Snake River Valley Quilt Guild in Idaho Falls, Idaho. This group's NQA grant helped fund a three-day Quilt Carnival focused on youth. Activities included hands-on learning centers, guided tours of the quilt show, and structured scavenger hunts to broaden and apply attendees' understanding of the art, techniques, and history of quilting.

Halfway across the country, the nonprofit Remus Area Historical Society in Michigan received another of NQA's 2014 grants. This group used its money to establish a quilt-block trail, which included structural quilt designs made by youth and adults. Each finished quilt board, painted and mounted on a barn somewhere in Mecosta County, reflected local traditions, culture, and history.

Another recipient in 2014 was EduQuilters of Satellite Beach, Florida. This grant helped fund numerous projects, including a children's summer quilt camp and a quilt-education conference. It also financed an ongoing community event known as Quilters Against Kids Hurting (QAKH), in which youth and adults make quilts for homeless children throughout the county. Sheryl Milner, QAKH coordinator, says of the quilters, "The women come here with no personal agenda whatsoever — except that they care about the children."

Indeed, the concept of caring seems to echo in all that National Quilting Association does, which explains quilters like Irene Goodrich, longtime NQA supporter. She pays her annual dues, attends chapter meetings, and donates Little Quilts — she has made twenty-seven of them, one for every year of the Little Quilt Auction.

Irene, born during the Great Depression, says she grew up with quilts. Her family's Virginia farmhouse didn't have central heat, so she and her seven brothers and sisters used quilts out of necessity. "My mother went to the general store and got their suit-sample books," she recalls. The pages of these books were actually 5-inch squares of wool appropriate for men's suits. "My mother made utility quilts out of them. She didn't quilt them, just tied them with a backing." Laughing, Irene says, "I tell you, those quilts were so heavy, they were a burden to sleep under! But they sure were warm."

From such rugged beginnings, Irene grew into a young adult and developed a love for appliqué. She made quilts for nieces and nephews, then for competitions and shows. "I've won over three hundred ribbons in state fairs and other places," she says. Now almost ninety years old and widowed, she makes and sells quilts "to pay the taxes each year." But that doesn't keep her from donating Little Quilts to the NQA.

Her small creation always stirs interest at the auction. For example, at the event's twenty-fifth anniversary, she contributed a 15-inch square Little Quilt with silver letters commemorating the anniversary. She included an intricately appliquéd bee in one corner, along with the NQA logo, finishing the work by hand quilting 12 to 14 stitches per inch.

Why go to so much trouble for a donated wall hanging? After all, Irene could've used that time to work on a quilt to sell for her own benefit. But her reason is simple: "I've just been a firm believer in the NQA," she explains. As a longtime member, she's bought into the philosophy of helping and caring, so that others can appreciate the art of quilting. She designs and creates her Little Quilts with that goal in mind, thus proving the premise that small things really do make a big difference.

Binding Stitch

You can be a part of the National Quilting Association! Check it out at www.nqaquilts.org. If your organization is considering applying for an NQA grant, see www.nqa quilts.org/grants/lqa/ for details, or write to the grant co-ordinator at grants@nqaquilts.org. To learn more about the EduQuilters, see www.eduquilters.org. For examples of barn-mounted quilt boards, go to www.facebook.com /RemusMuseum. Numerous other barn quilts are scattered around the country. For example, western North Carolina's Yancey and Mitchell Counties have over two hundred of them. You might want to read the book *Barn Quilts and the American Quilt Trail Movement* (Swallow Press, 2012), by Suzi Parron with Donna Sue Groves, mother of the barn-quilt movement.

DEMETRA'S QUILT

To a casual observer, Demetra looks like your typical California college student: long, loose hair, backpack slung over one shoulder, and a ready smile with a hint of stress — thanks to exams, extracurricular activities, homework, and a part-time job.

But if you look below the surface, you'll see something hidden, something that makes twenty-year-old Demetra different from most of her peers. She's a former foster kid who aged out of the system when she turned eighteen. Somehow, she managed to beat the odds and set goals for herself.

So why's that such a big deal? What happens to a foster kid who's too old for foster care? Ideally, he or she moves out of the foster family's home, finds a place to live, gets a job or enrolls in college, opens a bank account, buys a car, establishes a community of caring friends, and does whatever else is typical of mature adults.

But the reality is often different, says Kim Christenson, a quilter in the Daytona Beach area. When foster kids age out of the system on their eighteenth birthday, they have no support structure that enables them to live independently. Instead, they might crash on someone's sofa or in someone's car, get involved in drugs — using or pushing or both — and become statistics long before they figure out how to be adults.

Kim rattles off the stats from memory:

25 percent become incarcerated.

60 percent become parents.

25 percent are homeless.

Less than 3 percent will ever earn a college degree.

Kim discovered the age-out problem when she began volunteering at a girls' juvenile detention center. Since 1987 she and her church group have held services and spent one-on-one time with detainees on a weekly basis. During those years, she's gotten to know scores of girls who've aged out of the foster system and who've tried to make it on their own — without success.

Coincidentally, Kim read the novel *The Language of Flowers* (Random House, 2011), based on the life of a foster child. Its author, Vanessa Diffenbaugh, had founded the Camellia Network, which offers resources, opportunities, and support to every youth aging out of foster care. Kim responded, joined the network, and learned more about how to make a difference, one foster child at a time.

Camellia Network presents practical solutions for persons interested in helping, such as job internships and professional enrichment experiences. But there's no mention of quilting on Camellia's website. Kim wondered if her hobby could fit into the mix.

Then she saw Demetra. Recalling the moment, she says, "When I looked at the profiles on the Camellia website, Demetra's face touched me. I saw that her dream was to become a cutter-draper on Broadway." Kim pauses for a soft laugh. "That was my profession for several years, so I immediately felt a link with her." In addition, she learned that Demetra was already in college, studying and working part-time as a costumer.

Kim wanted to show Demetra that someone cared about her and her career goals. Someone knew she'd struggled and worked to make it to college. Someone was cheering for her as she pursued her dreams. A quilt, of course, would be a tangible reminder that Demetra had friends.

Kim and Jean Roth lead the Community Service Project of the Racing Fingers Quilters, and they enlisted several members to make a quilt. "From the book *The Language of Flowers*," Kim says, "I learned that flowers can be like a secret code in a quilt. You can tell a story in flowers." For example, quilters have known for years that roses represent love, and honeysuckle speaks of devotion. Besides, says Kim, "I love the Baltimore Album style of quilt, because of its messages in flowers." So Kim asked the women to create a flower quilt to depict purity, beauty, and resurrection.

They chose the Calla Lily pattern and did appliqué, piecing, and quilting. When finished, the beautiful quilt seemed worthy of someone special, and a few of its creators hesitated to hand it over to a former foster kid. "We can't give this to just anyone," one member stated through clenched teeth. "We don't want it ending up in somebody's garage sale."

Kim assured the quilters that her chosen recipient was indeed worthy, convincing them — even though she'd never met Demetra in person — that the young woman would treasure their efforts. The group finally agreed and sent the quilt, along with a card full of personal encouragement and well-wishes, to Demetra.

When the Sacramento chapter of Camellia Network presented the quilt to Demetra, she could hardly speak. For perhaps the first time in her life, she realized that a group of people loved and cared about her future, and she had a base of support — maybe even more support than your typical college student with loose hair and a backpack slung over one shoulder.

Demetra still gushes about the Calla Lily quilt. In an email correspondence, she says, "I must tell you that I take that quilt everywhere. I am so proud of it. I take it to work when the shop is cold to keep me warm while I sew. I take it to the park when I paint faces, make balloon animals, and play my ukulele for the children. I ask them to choose a flower on the quilt and make a kind wish for whoever made that flower so beautiful."

She works part-time as a professional faerie for a company called Happily Ever Laughter Parties, which arranges picnics and tea parties. At Demetra's events the quilt often holds a place of honor. "It so perfectly fits my personality that I wish I could explain it to you!" Writing directly to the quilters, she concludes, "Thank you, all of you, for this stunning invaluable gift you have given me."

Binding Stitch

Learn more about Racing Fingers Quilt Guild's charity work at www.racingfingersquiltguild.com/charity.htm. Learn more about the Camellia Network (a.k.a. the LifeSet Network) and meet dozens of former foster kids at www.camellia network.org.

Charity at Home and Beyond

It's autumn in eastern Washington state. Gusts of wind scatter red, yellow, and brown leaves in every direction, and a light rain dots the windowpanes. But regardless of the weather, inside Spokane's Beautiful Savior Lutheran Church every other Monday afternoon is quilt time. The women gather in the fellowship hall and spread fabric and batting on banquet tables. Then Phyllis Larsen and her friends pull out scissors and plug in sewing machines.

They have two ongoing projects, both with never-ending needs. First is Lutheran World Relief, which distributes homemade quilts to women and children in poverty-stricken villages around the globe. LWR, discussed in detail in the section "Unlikely Quilters," depends on volunteers like these for a steady production of bedcovers to keep up with demand. Phyllis and the group make most of their quilts with 11-inch squares of assorted donated materials. "We use whatever we get," she says with a laugh. "Seersucker, polyester, cotton — anything is fine for us."

While two people arrange forty-eight squares into a pleasing pattern on the floor — usually in diagonal rows of similar colors — two or three others sit at machines, ready to stitch the blocks together. When finished, a quilt top is layered onto a batting and backing on a large rectangular table, where a few other volunteers make quick work of tying it with colorful yarn. Another person then folds and machine-sews the edge of the backing onto the front edge, all around, for an easy binding.

They work for a couple of hours this autumn afternoon and will continue twice monthly, throughout the year, to complete as many quilts as possible for Lutheran World Relief. But they have another objective, one that illustrates the phrase "Charity begins at home." They make twin-bed quilts for all high-school graduates from their church.

"We have two reasons for doing this," says longtime quilter Becky Lucke. "First, we want a connection between them and the church." She acknowledges that some teens drift away from church attendance as they approach their college years, and she believes a quilt can remind them of their earlier commitments. A second motive follows logically, Becky says. "We want to show the graduates that we're there for them — that we care for them."

The graduates' quilts are made to be used and washed and used again. As Phyllis describes, "College kids can be hard on quilts, so we make them sturdy!" Yet there's also a gentler aspect to each quilt. Phyllis attaches a label she designed by computer with the student's confirmation Bible verse, his or her name, the church name, and the date of presentation.

In early June, the quilters hold a reception. All graduates, upon receiving their quilts, tell about their plans and dreams for the future. They also read their confirmation verses printed on the labels and offer a word of thanks to the quilters, who then send them on their way with a blessing.

In the months afterward, those quilts travel with graduates to college dorms or apartments. Grace Pochis, a 2013 grad, has taken her quilt to Willamette University in Salem,

Oregon, where she majors in history. She says, "I was honored that a group of people had put so much effort into something just for me. I didn't have a personal relationship with all of them, and yet I was receiving a gift from them."

Likewise, Thor Tangvald, who graduated from high school in 2011, took his quilt to his college — the University of Washington, and later to Washington State University. He even considered taking it on his year of study abroad in Spain, but, he says, "It is bulky, and I didn't have room for it in the bags I took."

Still, he thinks fondly of the quilt and the women who pieced it in dark colors with panthers and basketballs. "It was a cool gift," he says. "I was happy to have been given something by the church to show my efforts. It has a Bible verse on it, yet is sports-themed, so it fits in anywhere." Anticipating a degree in business and finance, Thor plans a career in law enforcement — perhaps working as a field agent with the FBI or DEA. Likely, his quilt will follow wherever his path leads.

Phyllis Larsen, one of the makers of Thor's quilt, had no idea years ago that her hobby would eventually bless other people. She started quilting in the early 1980s, almost on a dare. "My son was an exchange student in Australia," she recalls. "When he got back, he kept talking about his Australian host mother's quilting. I took that as a hint. Now all I do is quilt."

And it's a good thing she does. Her group touches lives in many ways and many places — from poverty-ridden children in faraway countries to high-school grads in their own backyard.

Binding Stitch

In your garden club, church, music association, or any other group, you probably have acquaintances with off-spring in high school. Why not start now and plan quilts for them when they graduate? A personalized quilt can link a young person to his or her roots, serving as a reminder of love, friendship, and home.

HISTORY DONE RIGHT

Do you love quilts? Do you love history?

You'll find a way to combine those loves with the American Quilt Study Group (AQSG), which dedicates its energy to encouraging, presenting, and preserving research on quilts and related textiles. Members also participate in quilt-making challenges, linking research to modern techniques and promoting interest in quilt history.

When most people think of the term "research," they might imagine a college professor in gray tweed, poring over dusty volumes in a library alcove. Or they think of an archaeologist in some foreign land, snapping photos of the ruins of a long-forgotten civilization. But when you merge the images, you might come up with a third: serious researchers delving into the world of quilts, which defines the mission of AQSG.

Membership in this organization allows persons the opportunity to provide a legacy for future generations. AQSG promises members that this legacy will honor those who came before them and the friends they make through their association with the organization. It goes on to say that members' commitment to quilting and quilt history reflects their interest in seeing research and documentation continue far into the future.

Such research takes place through grants and scholarships from the AQSG. For example, the Lucy Hilty Grant promotes research on quilt documentation, quilt-maker stories, textile production, and the quilting industry. Similarly, the H. Mark Dunn Research Grant Fund supports outstanding and innovative scholarship in quilt-related studies that impact the documenting of quilt textiles and the industry.

Slackers need not apply. That's because this involves serious research and serious educational endeavors. But there's serious fun too. AQSG offers scholarships for persons wanting to attend its annual seminar. Held in a different location every year, the event draws enthusiasts and scholars for a weekend dedicated to quilts. Besides hearing presentations and scholarly papers, attendees participate in preconference tours, roundtable discussions, and study sessions — all focused on quilts and quilt lovers. In addition, the weekend offers books on quilt history, auctions of quilt treasures, show-and-tell sessions, quilt exhibitions, and the sale of vintage quilts, textiles, and sewing tools from antiques dealers. The website declares, "AQSG's Seminar guarantees a unique learning experience for everyone with a connection to quilts."

Another draw for quilt scholars is AQSG's prestigious magazine, *Uncoverings*. Since 1980, this annual volume has served as a leading authority on quilt history and research. Again, no slackers here. The writer must prepare an article of 4,900 to 9,000 words (between twenty and thirty-five typed pages). Next, the article will undergo a thorough vetting by editors. They use a standard set of criteria, including these considerations:

- Does the paper make a significant contribution to the field?
- Is the scholarship sound, valid, and convincing?

- Is the paper well organized and engaging?
- Is the paper ready for publication with little editing necessary?

Five readers study each submission to *Uncoverings* using a "blind" system; that is, they don't know the name of the writer. If, after these editors' scrutiny, the submitted article is accepted for publication, the writer will be invited to attend the next annual AQSG seminar and present her research to the entire group. What's the likelihood of being published? Good — if you submit a worthwhile article. The website states, "A well-written, well-organized paper based on thorough, original research on a quilt-related topic and citing appropriate resources has an excellent chance of being accepted."

But even if you're not interested in submitting a scholarly article to *Uncoverings*, and even if you're not able to attend the AQSG's annual seminar, you can still be a part of this group, which encourages research and documentation of quilts old and new. Who knows? One day in the distant future, one of *your* quilts might be featured and discussed in a research paper.

That's a quilt history you could really love.

Binding Stitch

The American Quilt Study Group appreciates members and donors. If you're interested in supporting this worthy, not-for-profit organization, learn more at www.american quiltstudygroup.org or www.facebook.com/AmericanQuilt StudyGroup/info?tab=page_info.

BRINGING
COMFORT WHEN
DISASTER STRIKES

QUILTING 911

"It's about the quilting community that reaches out and says we are 100 percent behind you and the community that is hurting." Thus Jean Kester describes her never-ending concern for first responders — those who help others in times of disaster.

In 2005, when Hurricanes Katrina and Rita destroyed lives and property along the Gulf Coast, Jean worked as a 911 dispatcher in Goodyear, Arizona. Upon hearing about Katrina, her first impulse was to "find a ride and go help." But her job, along with college classes and three grandchildren in her care, wouldn't allow that kind of involvement. Instead, her husband suggested making quilts for first responders. Of course!

Most media focus on the victims of the tragedy — and rightly so. To a slightly lesser extent, we hear stories of firefighters and police officers on the front lines. But what about dispatchers? Almost always ignored, they are the true first responders; they take the calls, send help, and coordinate emergency teams.

Because Jean is herself a retired dispatcher — also known as a telecommunications officer — she understands their plight. After the 2005 hurricanes, she made quilts for a whole unit of dispatchers on the Gulf Coast. She also made a quilt for a New Orleans dispatcher who was separated from her baby during the storm's aftermath. And she made a quilt for a dispatcher in Pass Christian, Mississippi, who escaped onto the roof of the library during Katrina.

But that was only the beginning. "I quilted," she says, "for those on duty during the Virginia Tech tragedy. I have sent quilts to dispatchers whose homes were involved in flooding in New York; to dispatch centers who have lost members of their family (and believe me, dispatch centers *are* families); to dispatchers enduring chemotherapy; to dispatchers' ill children, premature children, fire victims, tornado victims."

With the tragic shooting in Aurora, Colorado, in 2012, she realized she could no longer handle the project by herself. She turned to social media, setting up a Facebook page. As a result, she says, "help came in droves. Quilters from all over the world sent so many quilts." She had enough to distribute to all dispatchers, first responders, and even the surviving victims and the families of those who had died in the shooting.

A few months later the shootings at Sandy Hook Elementary School grabbed the spotlight, and Jean asked for quilts through the internet. "Once again, the need was met," she says.

When yet another tragedy occurred — this time the loss of nineteen firefighters in Yarnell, Arizona, Jean decided to set up a more formal and permanent online group. Layers of Hope–Quilting 911 was born. Jean, the quilters, and their families have come to recognize the importance of quilting and sharing, transforming them all into more compassionate individuals.

If possible, Jean travels to the location of the tragedy and meets the dispatchers and others who were affected. Talking with them and seeing the devastation firsthand, she sometimes feels overwhelmed. Yet as she pulls quilts out of her van, the sorrow becomes a rallying point. She and the locals form a bond, and she realizes once again that she has been blessed in the giving.

An example occurred in the Northwest, in a little community Jean says she'd never heard of until tragedy struck. She's referring to Oso, Washington, where a mudslide engulfed fifty homes over a square mile of beautiful countryside in March 2014. Forty-three people died, and countless lives were turned upside down. More than a hundred first responders arrived on the scene, with dispatchers working overtime to coordinate the efforts. In all, some six hundred people helped with rescue and recovery.

Jean and her online group donated 376 quilts and numerous fleece blankets to Oso. Because of the large number of donations, she distributed them not only to dispatchers, but also to others who worked behind the scenes after the mudslide, such as the pastors ministering to first responders and families.

The quilting continues, because Jean never knows when the next tragedy will strike. Another mass shooting? More hurricanes? Devastating fires? Whatever the case, she and scores of online quilters will respond from around the country and around the globe.

As they respond, they identify with the people affected by the damage. Jean quotes her granddaughter after a visit to Oso. When asked by a young friend why she'd gone, the preteen answered, "Because our community had a landslide, and they really need us to help out and give back."

"*Our* community?" Jean thought. "We don't live anywhere near Oso!"

But when she considered more carefully, she realized

that, in a sense, everyone who cares can identify with a community that's hurting. That's why she continues to make and distribute quilts. That's why she continues to give.

Binding Stitch

Layers of Hope–Quilting 911's mission is to enhance the lives of 911 telecommunications operators (dispatchers) and their families during times of illness, disaster, loss, and tragedy by inspiring hope, faith, and optimism with a quilt of warmth and comfort in order to make a positive influence in the lives of those who make a difference every day, one quilt and one stitch at a time. If you'd like to make a quilt for Layers of Hope, contact Jean Kester on her blog (http://layersofhopequilting911.blogspot.com).

A Group of Friends

When a resident on Salt Spring Island, British Columbia, receives a large gift bag wrapped in yellow with a huge bow, he or she knows it's a mixed blessing. On the one hand, the gift indicates the recipient is sick — seriously. Cancer or some other life-threatening malady necessitates relentless treatments and countless visits to doctors, chemo appointments, and dialysis. On the other hand, the gift speaks of friends around the island — friends who have taken time to gather materials and meet, to cut, iron, stitch, quilt, bind, and deliver this labor of love.

Gwen Denluck, a quilter for thirty-five years, serves as one of seven coordinators for Island Comfort Quilts (ICQ), an informal group from many walks of life. Once a year they organize a community-wide quilting bee. They publicize the event in print and online, and approximately 150 preregistered people show up at the designated location, usually a large church's fellowship hall. Local merchants and individuals donate material and cash to ensure a smooth, welcoming environment for all volunteers.

During the one-day bee, workers position themselves at various stations. Production marches along in assembly-line fashion: from cutting tables to sewing machines to ironing boards. By the end of the day, Gwen admires a stack of thirty to forty completed lap quilts tied with yarn; they are then folded and placed in cloth bags. She and the ICQ members coordinate the distribution.

Like most charitable groups, the ICQ began when someone noticed a need. Gwen looks back and recalls, "The original organizer was diagnosed with breast cancer, and she received a quilt from Victoria Comfort Quilts, a national organization. She was so touched by receiving the quilt, she gathered a group of her friends and two people from the local quilt guild to discuss starting a group to make quilts for people on Salt Spring Island." This handful of organizers considered affiliating with the national group, but for various reasons decided to stay local.

A quilt top by Island Comfort Quilters, ready to be finished and donated to a sick or injured person in the community.

Their next step involved funding. They wrote letters to merchants and businesses around the island, requesting gifts of cash or supplies. When a newspaper article helped spread the word, donations poured in. The group then organized its first bee, and over a hundred volunteers came, ready to offer a variety of skills to accomplish the task.

Gwen points out, "The quilts are given to anyone with a life-threatening illness or injury, not just cancer." Along with the quilt in the bag, ICQ members include a card to the recipient listing the names of all who helped make the quilt. In addition, the local choir has donated copies of its CD to be tucked into the quilt bag. The music, says Gwen, particularly appeals to "people struggling with terminal illness, to help them heal."

Gwen recalls the example of a woman, diagnosed with breast cancer, who went for her first chemotherapy session. At the clinic she noticed many other patients with quilts and wished the same for herself. With a smile, Gwen says, "When she returned home, the quilt, wrapped beautifully, was waiting for her on her table. She took the quilt to every chemo [after that] and found solace in thinking of all the people who made it."

Indeed, the "mixed blessing" of a quilt gift somehow manages to overshadow the illness, and that's the hope of Island Comfort Quilts.

Binding Stitch

Practically anyone can start a charity quilt group like ICQ by gathering a few like-minded quilters and agreeing on recipients: accident victims, persons with terminal illnesses, or any other set of people. Keeping the group small at the beginning will allow it to grow without becoming overwhelmed. To see photos from Island Comfort Quilts, go to www.google.com/search?q=ISLAND+COM FORT+QUILTS&es_sm=122&tbm=isch&tbo=u& source=univ&sa=X&ei=Q_ayU4KZJsHxoAScpoKoD w&ved=0CDsQsAQ&biw=1280&bih=899.

Photo on page 171 courtesy of Gwen Denluck.

DANGER IN THE LINE

Crash! Bang! Teens at the Santa Cruz beach birthday party turned toward the sound and saw sparks. Expecting fireworks, many ran a few steps inland for a better look. One in the group, Jacob Kirkendall, noticed a small fire in the brush.

Already interested in becoming a firefighter, Jacob knew he could put out the blaze quickly. But a snapped power line attacked him in the near darkness. Twenty-two thousand volts of electricity surged into his head and through his body.

His friends called 911 when they heard him scream in pain and then saw him pass out. When firefighters arrived, one made a daring rescue, pulling the seventeen-year-old away from the live wire. Other first responders rushed the boy to the hospital. There, the doctors' dire prognoses included a variety of life-altering possibilities, like amputation of a hand and a foot. In fact, medical personnel saw little reason for optimism. One surgeon emphatically stated, "He shouldn't be breathing; he shouldn't be breathing!"

That night began a hellish ordeal: ten weeks in a medically induced coma; second- and third-degree burns; eighteen surgeries on the skull, hand, and arm; pneumonia, infections, and skin grafts. Thanks to prayers and many medical procedures, Jacob eventually awoke, having no memory of that June 28, 2009, event.

Throughout his four months in various hospitals, Jacob

and his family discovered friends, old and new, who offered support. Some organized fund-raisers. Some brought gifts like decorated walking sticks. Hundreds sent get-well cards. Firefighters presented a department sweatshirt and a signed helmet. And a group of women made a quilt.

Janet Hames, a member of the Santa Clara Valley Quilt Association (SCVQA), participates in a twelve-person circle within the guild. "We call it 'Our Little Quilt Group,'" she explains. "We're not really formal; we just meet to quilt." And they do plenty of that during their gatherings in various members' homes. "We have a lot of fun in our group," Janet says. "Some [people] are cutting, some are sewing." Once a year they focus on charity work, including making hundreds of cuddle quilts for local Ronald McDonald Houses, raffle quilts for high-school fund-raisers, cozy quilts for cancer patients, and numerous other donations.

Our Little Quilt Group made Jacob's quilt in bright colors depicting some of his favorite activities, such as surfing and biking.

The volunteers in the larger SCVQA prepare quilt kits, which members piece into a variety of quilts. Once that's done, participants in the Little Quilt Group hold a quilt-a-thon, where they finish dozens of quilts in a short period of time.

When Nancy Toombs, a member of the group, told

them about Jacob's accident, Janet and the others dropped their other work and planned a new project. Nancy, a family friend for years, knew Jacob as an active, outdoorsy guy — he loved surfing and fixed-gear biking, for example — so she suggested blocks to reflect his interests. Each member created a 12-inch block, and the group stitched them into a brightly colored twin quilt.

Jacob left the hospital still with "a pretty big dent" in his head, he recalls, but immediately he focused on recovery. When Nancy took the finished quilt to Jacob's home, she learned he was away — working hard at physical therapy. Disappointed to have missed him, she left the quilt with his aunt, believing that the family — and Jacob — would treasure it.

In the weeks that followed, she discovered Jacob's stamina knew no bounds. Wearing a helmet, he started driving again and went back to high school. He graduated with his class and was able to walk across the stage to receive his diploma, "an awesome experience," he says. The firefighter who had rescued him from the power line began mentoring him after graduation, as Jacob took firefighting classes — a big step toward fulfilling his career dream.

Through the whole ordeal, Jacob Kirkendall felt the help and support of many, including the daring firefighter, friends and strangers, concerned quilters, and even God himself, who answered the prayers of many people. Looking back, he says, "It was really neat to see God working in all this."

Binding Stitch

Jacob's story has many facets beyond the quilt from Nancy and Janet and the Little Quilt Group. He recently married and is studying to be a firefighter — and he's still surfing. To see Jacob and hear his own account of the accident and the long road to recovery, go to http://player.vimeo.com /video/31442193. To read blog posts from Jacob's father, a pastor in California, see www.journeythroughfire.blogspot .com. To learn more about Nancy and Janet's Santa Clara Valley Quilt Association, go to www.scvqa.org.

Photo on page 174 courtesy of Nancy Toombs.

CHEMO QUILTS

For years, Adele Carter, of Spokane, Washington, has been making quilts for children with cancer — Chemo Quilts, she calls them. But when faced with the same diagnosis herself, she understood the kids' plight firsthand. Without hesitation she now declares, "Those children are the bravest little people I've seen in my life."

Adele, at age eighty, recalls learning to quilt from her grandmother, who pieced and quilted all by hand. Most of the family's bedcovers comprised scraps from dresses, shirts, and aprons. Adele's early attempts, like her grandmother's, were scrappy. Even today, she says, her own children glance at those old quilts and recognize pieces from blouses or other clothing.

In the mid-1990s Adele's quilting took a surprising turn. A woman in her Washington State Quilters group had been coordinating the donation of quilts for children at a Spokane hospital. Adele says, "She asked if I would make a quilt for a little girl. So I did." But Adele didn't realize the coordinator herself had health problems until a few days later. "She called again and asked me to take over her position until she felt better."

Agreeing to a short-term job, Adele accepted the woman's phone list and started making contacts. Weeks turned into months, however, and the coordinator's health continued to decline. That's when Adele figured short-term had morphed into long-term.

But she's not complaining. She's grown to love the job,

along with the forty women who work with her to piece and quilt for these children. She says her group has made over five hundred quilts — all custom designs. The hardest part is getting started. "When I get the call from the hospital, I just hate hearing that another child has cancer." But she stops, prays, and then feels ready to start working. "The rest is pure pleasure," she declares.

Her first step is to talk with the hospital about the family's request. Is the child interested in a hobby? A cartoon character? School colors? Younger kids are fairly predictable. Girls usually like flowers, butterflies, and princesses; boys often prefer trucks, airplanes, and wild animals. Some older kids have unique requests, she notes — like a logo for the rock band KISS or the mascot of a professional basketball team from the opposite side of the country — "but we have never failed to give the children what they wanted."

Next, Adele makes the quilt herself or calls on one of her volunteers. "I know their talents and interests. Some of my quilters like challenging projects; others prefer something simple." She tries to match the child's request with the quilter's skills.

In some cases, a child is too young to make a request. Adele remembers a particular family whose baby daughter clung to life. "The parents were from Turkey, and the specialist called to ask me how quick I could make a quilt." Adele and her volunteers usually produce a quilt in less than a month, but this case seemed extremely urgent. "It was a Thursday night," Adele recalls, "and the parents wanted a white quilt with an angel on it." With hardly a pause, Adele remembers promising, "How about Monday?" The grateful specialist comforted the family with this news.

"The next morning," Adele says, "I got started. I found a cute pattern with an angel with outstretched arms. I got that appliquéd on Friday." She then called a longarm quilting volunteer, who picked up the top and quilted it on Saturday. Adele added a binding on Sunday, and the quilt reached the family, as promised, on Monday morning. The baby lived only one week longer.

Yes, Adele's job includes sorrow, but it also has lighter moments. A few years ago she got a request for a quilt featuring angry birds. Scratching their heads, Adele and her volunteers tried to imagine birds with emotional issues. Crows squawking at a farmer? Vultures failing to locate their prey? After some discussion, Adele and a couple of quilters asked the clerk at a sewing store, where they learned about the video game by that name and with a laugh bought official Angry Birds fabric.

Each Chemo Quilt is unique, created specifically to meet the child's request. This one features famous Thomas & Friends™ images, along with other trains, for a four-year-old. (Quilt made and photographed by the author.)

Even though the work is "pure pleasure," Adele recently faced a hurdle. She was diagnosed with cancer and found herself going through the same procedures as the children who receive her quilts. Surgery, radiation, chemotherapy, blood tests, and an unending cycle of doctor visits. That's when she observed firsthand how children appreciated her creative work. "These kids take the quilts home with them," she observes, "and when they come back, they bring the quilts with them. Everywhere they go, they take the quilts; they're getting a lot of comfort from them."

As soon as possible after recovering, Adele went back to quilting as therapy. She's made bedcovers and throws for numerous charities, but she keeps returning to the Chemo Quilts. She likes the personal touch of the custom work. "Right from the beginning," she says, "you know the name of the child, you're saying prayers for that child, and that child is in your mind." It's a personalized quilt that shows love and care.

"I won't stop, as long as I can thread a needle and talk on the phone," Adele declares. "These quilts bring a lot of joy in a difficult time."

Yes, joy for the quilter, and joy for the "bravest little people" who receive them.

Binding Stitch

You too can become a Chemo Quilt volunteer. Check with your local quilt group or shop to see if anyone else has the same goal. Or speak with a hospital chaplain or volunteer coordinator, who will get you started in this area of service.

COMMUNITY
STITCHING

Your grandmother probably did it; your great-grandmother surely did. Every spring they faced the daunting task of washing quilts in a wringer machine or in a tub of boiling water. But they knew most bedding didn't get that dirty and the harsh treatment of washing would shorten the quilt's life. Also, the labor-intensive effort of handling wet quilts would tax even the hardiest of souls. That's why most women a hundred years ago chose another method of freshening their bedcovers after a long winter: airing the quilts.

Come spring, women removed quilts from the beds, a few at a time, and draped them over clotheslines on sunny days. The cool, clean breeze permeated the quilts and took away the mustiness from a long winter of use. Unless the quilts showed obvious signs of dirt, the airing sufficed, and after a day in the sunshine the quilts were folded and stored until autumn.

In recent years, by contrast, quilt owners have found numerous methods of refreshing their quilts. Some prefer vacuuming, while others choose dry cleaning. Some follow great-grandma's washtub process, filling a bathtub with lukewarm water and gentle detergent and then swishing the quilt by hand. They wash, drain the tub (while the quilt remains), and then fill again for a rinse. After another rinse and drain, they press out as much water as possible (without wringing) and spread the quilt on a sheet on the lawn to dry naturally.

That may be the best method for older quilts, but most new ones can hold up to a romp in the washing machine. Experts agree that quilts should be washed with a liquid detergent — unscented, color-free, and without fabric softener or bleach. Beyond that, a regular cycle with warm water will do, and putting the quilt through another complete cycle — using cold water this time, without detergent — will ensure a thorough rinsing. Most modern quilts can also withstand a clothes dryer set on "warm." In lieu of using a dryer, the quilts can be spread out on sheets in the yard, just as great-grandma did. (Avoid the direct sunlight, though, to keep them from fading!)

The Airing of the Quilts, by the Tall Pines Quilt Guild, Huntsville, Texas.

But let's go back to airing. One group in Huntsville, Texas, is dedicated to this process. Since 2002, the Tall Pines Quilt Guild (TPQG) has held a public biannual Airing of the Quilts downtown, in an area designated by Texas as an official cultural district. Quilts — new and antique — hang around the courthouse balcony and along the streets surrounding the town square. The first Saturday in May, every other year, has been designated "Airing Day," and the city hosts a complementary festival.

The event accomplishes several goals. First, it raises the public's awareness of and appreciation for quilts. It also educates, encourages, and preserves the heritage and future of quilting. And it lets people know about the guild's charitable work.

Since the group's founding in 1984, Tall Pines members have made and donated quilts to numerous charities, such as an orphanage in Russia, the local Pregnancy Care Center, Habitat for Humanity, Child Protective Services, and the Huntsville Memorial Hospital. In fact, in 2003 they made and sold a Pink Ribbon quilt to raise money for the Huntsville Hospital Mammogram Fund and the underinsured women of Walker County. A year later, the guild stitched a replica quilt and donated it to the hospital, where it still hangs in the entry hall.

According to a newsletter account, the Tall Pines Charity Bee donates about ninety quilts a year to local organizations. When the bee was formed, it had only one focus: to make baby quilts for the Pregnancy Care Center, says chairperson Robin Rodriquez. This focus has continued over the

(Left to right) Robin Rodriquez, Susan Craig, and Jane Richmond sort HUGS quilts for the Tall Pines charities.

years. "We give them a baby shower every January," Robin declares.

But the bee's scope has broadened to include several other charities as well. Bee members make small items to donate, including wall hangings and walker caddies. Among its most quirky projects are pillows stuffed with scraps and batting. When crammed full, they support nursing home patients who sit in wheelchairs, or they prop up arms or legs wherever needed.

The Airing of the Quilts event gives the public an opportunity to become aware of TPQG's charitable work in the community. As visitors and locals stroll through downtown, they admire the displays and shop at vendors' booths and a special general store sponsored by the guild. There they find homemade items to purchase, thereby supporting the guild and its work.

And the guild's work covers a lot of territory and skill levels. For example, anyone can make a kid's quilt, which members call HUGS, says Robin. "We make them for kids, in various sizes, and we make them all year," she says. Once annually, the bee sorts them by size and theme. Then Robin distributes them to several local charities. The guild also gives a scholarship each year to a deserving student in math or fiber arts. Other recipients of TPQG's generosity include Saafe House, a women's shelter, which gives quilts at Christmas; Child Protective Services; Head Start; Good Shepherd Food Bank; Boys and Girls Clubs; and the Girl Scouts.

It's easy to imagine your great-grandmother wiping her hands on her apron and smiling at TPQG's charity work. She'd be pleased that its members care about their community. And she'd feel right at home at the Airing of the Quilts. In fact, if invited, she might even air a few of her own.

Binding Stitch

Consider how you can use a public event, such as a quilt show or other crafting fair, to involve passersby in your guild's charities. You can set up a drop-off bin for donated fabric and supplies. Just be sure to promote your charity events ahead of time, so that visitors will be prepared to donate. Or have a demonstration area for tying quilts for the homeless shelter and invite visitors to join the work. Check out Tall Pines Quilt Guild at www.tallpinesquiltguild.com. If you're interested in washing a quilt, you can find good advice at numerous websites or at your local quilt shop. The information above came from www.quilting101.com /care/quilt-washing. The shop Fabric Carousel in Huntsville (www.fabriccarousel.com) partners with TPQG in much of its charity work.

Photo on page 183 courtesy of Tall Pines Quilt Guild. Photo on page 184 courtesy of Robin Rodriquez.

GEE'S BEND QUILTERS

Word spread quickly in Gee's Bend, Alabama: a crazy white man paid good money to buy raggedy old quilts. The year was 1998, and the crazy man was William Arnett. While researching African American vernacular art, he'd stumbled across a photo of a stunning quilt with a design made out of red and orange bars. More research led him to the home of Annie Mae Young.

She greeted him on her porch and studied the photo with a frown, thinking maybe she'd burned that quilt the week before. After all, neighbors for miles around knew that smoke from burning cotton drove off mosquitoes. Women often used their older quilts this way.

But Annie Mae, seeing the distress on Arnett's face, decided to look around her house, in cabinets, closets, and under-bed storage. Finally she found the very quilt he'd been seeking. She offered it to the man, free of charge, but Arnett would have none of it. He wrote her a generous check, and she threw in an armload of other quilts to sweeten the deal.

Annie Mae gained a few thousand dollars that day. The United States gained a historical treasure.

Gee's Bend, sixty miles southwest of Montgomery in a peninsular bend in the Alabama River, boasts a population of 275, according to the 2010 census. The town was named for its founders, the Gee family, who settled there in the early 1800s. In 1845 Mark Pettway bought the land,

and after the Civil War freed slaves moved to this isolated peninsula. Many newcomers even took the name Pettway as their own.

Residents lived peacefully, coming and going across the river by ferry, into the early 1960s. Many of them also used that ferry to attend civil rights and voting rights activities, which caught the attention of local authorities. As a result, ferry transportation was suspended, and Gee's Bend lost its direct route to the outside world.

Authorities made no apology or explanation for disruption of ferry service, except for a terse, chilling statement from Sheriff Lummie Jenkins: "We didn't close the ferry because they were black. We closed it because they forgot they were black."

But Gee's Bend residents discovered new ways to press on. Led by civil rights worker and Episcopalian priest Francis X. Walter, they founded the Freedom Quilting Bee in 1966 to provide income for the community. In fact, for a few years the bee sold quilts to Bloomingdale's, Sears, and other stores. Quilters used the money to buy twenty-three acres of land and build a bigger facility for producing quilts and other handicrafts, like potholders, placemats, and aprons. One part of the building brought in additional income as a day-care center. In another positive turn, eight families who had been evicted from their homes because they'd registered to vote bought parcels of this property and settled there.

Amazingly, a full forty-four years passed before ferry service was restored. Gee's Bend blossomed then, already enjoying fame from William Arnett's discovery of the quilts. That same year — 2006 — the U.S. Postal Service issued a series of stamps featuring Gee's Bend's colorful quilts, and by 2008 the town had erected a Quilt Mural Trail. This walking tour, reminiscent of Boston's Freedom Trail, showcases several quilts in dazzling outdoor displays. It begins at the Freedom Quilting Bee and continues through town, marking quilters' homes, the old community school, and the ferry terminal.

But the quilts needed — no, demanded — a larger audience. Thanks to Arnett, museums across the country clamored to display Gee's Bend quilts. Throughout the first decade of the twenty-first century, seventy of them, including six made by Annie Mae Young, traveled to Houston, Atlanta, San Francisco, New York, Indianapolis, and Philadelphia.

Art critics lavished praise. Michael Kimmelman, in the *New York Times*, described the quilts as "some of the most miraculous works of modern art America has produced." He went on to call them "eye-poppingly gorgeous." Peter Marzio, director of the Museum of Fine Arts in Houston, declared, "All I know is that the museum's a better place because of the Gee's Bend exhibitions. They expand the sense of what art can be." Mark Stevens, of *New York* magazine, said, "The strikingly beautiful quilts just might deserve a place among the great works of twentieth-century abstract art."

With such effusive praise, the women of Gee's Bend experienced overnight success and an immediate demand for their work. Some quilts have fetched as much as $20,000 each, while many more cost a modest $1,000. An individual quilt block, which can be framed or stitched into a larger quilt, costs around $30.

Although these prices may seem high to the uninitiated,

quilters themselves know the hours required to make a full-size bedcover: choosing fabric, cutting, piecing, layering, quilting, and binding. Added to the cost of labor and materials is the irrepressible artistic quality. Who can put a price on that? Besides, the proceeds have not been squandered. The Gee's Bend Quilters Collective helps distribute and manage the income. Part of each sale goes directly to the quilt maker, some goes to the other members, and then some to the collective for expenses.

What kind of future do Gee's Bend residents envision? With help from architecture students at Auburn University, they see a thriving community that attracts tourists and offers a variety of activities. Professor Sheri Schumacher says a Gee's Bend Learning Center will provide guest housing as well as the opportunity to study quilting and other local history. Even more events will draw additional tourists: paddling the Alabama River, fly-fishing for fun or competition, and biking the wilderness trails. The community already welcomes visitors for its May Day Celebration, which includes quilting, food, parades, music, and a traditional Maypole dance.

So the story of Gee's Bend is a story of quilts. Quilts served as a catalyst for growth; quilts sustained during difficult times; quilts will help lead residents into the future.

Maybe that white guy wasn't so crazy after all.

Binding Stitch

You can help Gee's Bend by visiting the town. From Montgomery, drive to the ferry for a short ride. Enjoy the sights, buy a quilt or other craft item, eat lunch, meet quilters, and watch them work. You won't regret your time in Gee's Bend. To learn more and see photos, check out the *Smithsonian* (www.smithsonianmag.com/arts-culture/fabric-of-their -lives); the Quilt Alliance online newsletter (www.alliance foramericanquilts.org); *Deep South Magazine* (www.deepsouth mag.com/2012/04/the-future-of-gees-bend); the Rural Development Leadership Network (www.ruraldevelopment.org /FQBhistory.html); and Gee's Bend on Facebook (www .facebook.com/QuiltsofGeesBend).

GIVING AND GIVING

ATTENTION AREA QUILTERS: The Giving Quilt,
Inc., needs you! So assemble your stash, grab your
rotary cutter, and start your sewing machines!

This news release, published in 2014, is typical of the ongoing appeal from a Louisiana charity. The Giving Quilt
(TGQ), a nonprofit, offers crafters of all skill levels the opportunity to make a quilt and donate it either to a charity
of their choice or to a general clearinghouse where TGQ
designates the recipient.

Unlike some quilt groups, TGQ began specifically as a
charitable entity. Its original mission focused on providing
quilts to wounded soldiers, but since those beginnings in
2008, the mission has expanded. It now donates to various organizations, such as a neonatal unit in Baton Rouge
and St. Jude's Children's Research Hospital in Memphis,
Tennessee. Also included are some lesser-known organizations: Child and Adolescent Bereavement Services in Baton
Rouge, supporting kids and teens who've lost a close relative to traumatic death; the Alzheimer's Disease Coopera-
tive Study, where Vietnam veterans participate as subjects
in a study on aging; and Adullam Household of Faith, a
home for children whose parents are incarcerated.

Renee Hoeprich, who's worked with TGQ since 2012,
believes the group has a place for volunteers of all ages. Her
interest lies in quilts made by children for children. For

years she was involved in designing and stitching more than 175 quilts for Project Linus through the PTA of her son's school, Forwood Elementary, in Encinitas, California. That led to the beginnings of her Kids Draw 4 Kids (KD4K) project at The Giving Quilt. "I've always been involved in crafts, even from the time I was a teenager," she says. Her kid-friendly program gives youngsters the opportunity to create artistic quilt blocks, which become part of child-size quilts donated to Louisiana charities. The KD4K booth always generates interest among young attendees. In April 2013, for example, it produced nine quilts at The Giving Quilt Show in Gonzales, sponsored by the National Quilting Association.

"But I can't draw!" some children moan. Renee responds with a smile and guides them in the use of fabric markers. Over the years, she's discovered almost any child can draw a sea creature, such as a jellyfish or turtle. She says the first-time experience of drawing on fabric usually delights kids, and they complete their quilt block with a sense of accomplishment.

The children who receive the quilts feel good too. Renee observes, "When those kids find out that children in the community made this [quilt] for them, they think it's really neat." At last count, more than thirty-two hundred children have drawn blocks for quilts at KD4K. Besides teaching kids the joy of giving, Renee says, "I've found a unique way to share our quilting heritage with a contemporary purpose."

Many KD4K events occur outside the usual quilting venues. Sharon Hicks, coordinator of Baton Rouge Quilts for Kids, worked with Jefferson Terrace Elementary School students to produce artwork for several quilts. And the Jones Creek Branch of the East Baton Rouge Parish Library System has hosted a KD4K event.

Although the Kids Draw 4 Kids project appeals to youngsters, The Giving Quilt overall aims to encourage adults — quilters of all skill levels — to donate quilts. TGQ sponsors sew days throughout the year as well as hands-on participation at its biennial show. Individuals and groups are welcome to share the love of quilting and giving. Participants may choose a particular charity to receive their quilts, or TGQ will distribute them as needed. At the 2013 show, more than 560 quilts were donated to twenty-five charitable organizations, and two additional Quilts of Valor were presented individually to local veterans.

Renee points out that TGQ's mission has not changed since its inception. "The National Quilting Association has informed us that, to their knowledge, we are the only quilt show that holds an event displaying only quilts for donation," she says. And, thanks to The Giving Quilt's presence on the web, she notes that participation has extended well beyond Louisiana. People in Iowa, California, and Mississippi have donated to TGQ. "We have received out-of-state quilts for every show and often receive fabric donations from out of state."

The Giving Quilt encourages groups to do their own giving, in conjunction with TGQ or independently, and one guild does just that: the Wasted Women's Bee (WWB) in Baton Rouge. Cofounders Judy Holley and Sherry Herringshaw, in a club newsletter, explain: "The Wasted Women's Bee works closely with TGQ. We are a group of dedicated local quilters who recycle donated fabric, unfinished projects, and sewing-room waste into quilts for charitable donations." They say WWB members "can't bear to see bits and pieces of good fabric thrown away, so they meet and sew the stray parts into quilts." Those quilts then go to numerous organizations, such as nursing homes, hospitals, and hospice centers.

In addition, if Wasted Women members notice a need outside their community, they make and donate quilts to that area. When floods devastated parts of Colorado in 2014, WWB collected dozens of quilts, pillowcases, and stuffed bears for distribution, and The Giving Quilt paid for shipping.

The guild encourages people to donate quilt tops to WWB. This kind of donation helps in more ways than one. Besides the eventual benefit to charity, Judy and Sherry say these tops "can be used by new quilters to learn machine quilting. Machine quilting is a skill that requires lots of practice, and the charity quilts are a good way for students to get the practice hours they need."

Like many other groups who make charity quilts, the WWB offers several avenues of service. "There are always donations to sort, quilts to bind, kits to cut, or borders to add," says Judy. Sometimes a member drops by, grabs a preassembled kit, and takes it home to sew later.

But whatever they're doing, it's all about helping people. In this, the Wasted Women's Bee reflects the philosophy of The Giving Quilt. "Assemble your stash, grab your rotary cutter, and start your machine" should be a rallying cry for quilters in Louisiana — and anywhere else — to use their skills for the benefit of others.

Binding Stitch

You can start your own informal charitable quilt group, or ask a clerk at your local quilt shop if she knows of a group already in existence. Or you can support The Giving Quilt and its work (www.thegivingquiltinc.org/donations). For great photos of donations to The Giving Quilt, see www .thegivingquiltinc.org/show-gallery. If you'd like more information about Wasted Women, you'll find it at www .thegivingquiltinc.org/wasted-women-bee. You can attend one of their meetings anytime. As Sherry says, "Joining the group is not difficult — you just show up!"

Start with a foundation fabric, 10 inches square. Place a 2-inch strip of another fabric diagonally across the center of this square. Sew strips of fabric — also known as strings — on either side of the center strip until the entire foundation is covered. Trim the resulting block to a 9½-inch square, and you've got the beginnings of a string quilt. It's that easy.

The concept of string quilts began almost two hundred years ago. African American slaves accumulated strips of fabric and pieced them together out of necessity to make functional bedcovers. In a similar way, frugal Amish women often made string quilts to use up their small pieces of fabric and avoid waste. Later, during America's Victorian craze, women collected cigar ribbons and pieced them into silky, decorative quilts. All three examples illustrate a similar piecing process. Today, quilters employ the same string technique for a variety of reasons, but mainly because it's a simple way to make a quilt, and the results can be stunningly dramatic.

For years, Mary Johnson and several online friends used the string-piecing method to help reduce their stashes — fabric that quilters usually have crammed into closets, stacked on bookshelves, and stuffed into shoeboxes. But an internet brainstorming session led Mary and the others to consider using the string technique for a higher purpose. As a result, the Heartstrings Quilt Project came about in 2007.

Mary, who lived in Minneapolis, Minnesota, at the

time, decided early in the brainstorming that she and her group didn't want the administrative headache of managing a central warehouse for collection and distribution. "We believed that we would have more success and make and donate more quilts if each member finishing the quilts was able to designate a recipient of her choice," she says. As a result, string quilts find homes with veterans, children in need, neighbors who've experienced disasters, and a variety of other groups and individuals.

To Mary, Heartstrings quilts are much more than stash-busters. "My passion for making and donating quilts to those in need comes from my personal experience. I saw the difference the comfort of a quilt I'd made brought to both my father-in-law and my aunt when they were sick and dying."

Her involvement in Heartstrings doesn't usually include meeting the recipients, but she believes the project is accomplishing its purpose. "I know that the work we're doing at Heartstrings is providing warmth and comfort to all those who receive our quilts."

She gives an example from an email thank-you she received. The note, she says, was written by "the daughter of a woman who was going to undergo surgery and chemotherapy for breast cancer. Her mother had spent her life volunteering and giving to others, and her daughter wanted her to have a quilt as she underwent treatment." A photo attached to the thank-you showed the mother with her quilt "and a big smile on her face," Mary says. "It was lovely to see."

Mary believes the sum of the parts is greater than individual components. From the start of Heartstrings, she says, she's wanted to encourage and support others in their volunteering, making her project a unified effort. "As a group, we're able to make and donate more quilts than we can as individuals."

Heartstrings offers simple instructions to make string blocks, and its website presents scores of photos. One look through the album will inspire any quilter's imagination. In addition, Mary has provided a variety of options for taking part in Heartstrings. Persons interested only in piecing can make any number of individual blocks or a whole string quilt top and send it to the address provided. Another volunteer will do the quilting and binding, and the finished bedcover will be donated from there. A second option allows a person to quilt or tie donated quilt tops. Even non-quilters can be involved in a third option: donating fabric for backing.

But there's a fourth option, one that should appeal to quilters in every community across the country. Start with a foundation fabric, 10 inches square. Place a 2-inch strip of another fabric diagonally…and eventually donate your string quilt to your favorite local charity.

Because Heartstrings really is that easy.

Binding Stitch

If you're looking for a user-friendly block to piece for charities, you won't go wrong with a string quilt. Look for inspiration at www.heartstringsquiltproject.com. You can find simple instructions and quilt patterns at Mary's website (www.maryquilts.com).

THE ROSEMORES

You could use the phrase "all in the family" or "family affair" if you were writing a newspaper headline about the Rosemores in Jenkins, Minnesota. But you'd never use "family feud." That's because, in spite of different personalities and careers, everyone in the clan unites in a love for quilting.

Start with the matriarch, Arlean. She began life in Madelia, Minnesota, dropped out of school, and married while still a teenager. After four children and eight grandchildren, she decided to "get her own things done," so she went back to school and graduated — fifty-two years behind her classmates.

In the midst of her busy life, she collected stories of her family's varied adventures, wrote two books, and coauthored a third. Along the way she also managed to instill a passion for her favorite pastime in her children — "all blue-ribbon quilters," she says proudly.

Consider her oldest, Dan, now a retired research scientist. His interest in quilting morphed over the years into a related hobby: working with fur. He's made a full-size Trip around the World quilt from a variety of furs, all of which had to be sewn by hand. He's also made faux-fur quilts using the same pattern.

And then there's daughter Ranae. Arlean says she's "a very accomplished designer of quilts." Though Ranae's day job involves working with the disabled, she spends her free time sewing. One of her quilts, depicting a motorcycle, is on display at a Harley Davidson museum in California. Recently, her quilting skills have led her into another area: making costumes. At the annual Renaissance Faire, members of the Rosemore family wear period outfits, thanks to Ranae's artistic skills.

A second daughter, Mary, worked for years as a contract builder. She built dozens of homes in Minnesota's Brainerd Lakes area, but, Arlean says, "when the housing market tanked, she decided that a quilt shop would be a way to make a living." The shop has done well since its beginnings in 2008, and Arlean believes this success is due to a combination of factors. "Mary has a very good business head, which is as important as being able to quilt." Like all of Arlean's children, Mary can quilt by hand. "I made them learn," says Mom, "and always told them they didn't have to hand-quilt for a living, but I wanted them to know how." Mary took that advice literally, and now she specializes in *machine* quilting. At any given moment her shop has forty to fifty tops layered and waiting to be quilted.

Don't forget the youngest of Arlean's children: Ralph, Jr. Like his siblings, he grew up with quilting. Arlean recalls with a laugh, "He did not like cutting blocks, but that was something they had to do, like it or not!" She admits that Ralph was good at hand quilting but never enjoyed it. To him, the best part of the process involves designing and putting colors together. Now in his mid-forties and a career military officer,

Children flock to the Rosemores' quilting booth at the Minnesota State Fair, eager to add artwork to quilt blocks for charity.

Ralph has seen three tours of duty in the Middle East. But when he comes home, he helps in the family's quilting projects.

A new generation of Rosemores has emerged as quilt enthusiasts also. Arlean's granddaughters, Cassie, Morena, and Dana, have won ribbons for artistic quilting and other sewing projects in 4-H competitions and county and state fairs.

Like the rest of the clan, they immerse themselves in the quilting tradition, which is especially evident each year in late August. That's when they gather in St. Paul for the Minnesota State Fair. For more than twenty-two years, Arlean and her offspring have staffed a booth on the first Sunday of the fair, with the goal of encouraging children to help make a quilt. Even Arlean's youngest grandchildren enjoy standing on an ice chest and showing quilt blocks to passersby. Best of all, Arlean says, "Parents love us. It is the only free thing for kids to do at the fair!" During a recent year, she says, about 275 kids approached the booth, where they were invited to color a picture. In turn, the artwork was ironed onto a quilt block, which was stitched to other blocks, layered, quilted, and given to a child in crisis.

But the Rosemores' charity work didn't start there. Arlean remembers a neighbor's tragedy in the mid-1980s. "The family had a house fire, and we made them each a quilt. The next year, there were two families, and so it went. Now we make and give away about three hundred quilts a year."

Even a large clan like the Rosemores might have problems producing that many quilts. Thankfully, a few others have become unofficial cousins and help when needed.

Arlean holds a regular quilting bee on Thursday afternoon and evening, and a handful of friends and neighbors show up along with family members. An even bigger event happens annually: the Rosemores' Quilt-a-Thon, which draws a crowd of forty to fifty in addition to family. They all meet at a church gymnasium in nearby Pequot Lakes. "We start about eight o'clock in the morning and make quilts until about seven or eight in the evening. People come and go all day," Arlean explains. "We make about seventy or eighty on that day."

She's thankful for her community's support. Even the small town of Jenkins itself, population 440, contributes storage space. Arlean says, "They have a tiny town hall, but they share it with us. I always like to praise them for giving us that space, when every town around us wanted to charge us many more dollars than we had. We get the use of it for free."

Though the Rosemore charity is not officially recognized, Arlean says generous people donate material, and they have never run out of fabric. That's a good thing, because one of their recent projects required lots of it. Granddaughter Morena, active in 4-H, heard from a neighbor about a fledgling school in Zulu Natal, South Africa, where most of its one hundred students had been orphaned because of AIDS. The school building had neither furniture nor supplies, and at night the children slept on a bare concrete floor. Morena responded with big plans: a quilt for each child. She appealed to quilt groups and churches, and soon piles of children's bedding filled a corner of Mary's shop. With help from several family members, Morena's 4-H club tied the quilts and added bindings. Donations

Children at the school in Zulu Natal, South Africa, now have quilts to use as bedding, thanks to the Rosemores.

from local businesses provided the money they needed to ship the quilts overseas.

This international project is impressive, and the Rosemores were happy to spearhead it. But they usually keep their donations closer to home. Arlean says, "Our policy of giving out our quilts is that there is only one person between us and the child who receives the quilt." This means she and her family are constantly on the lookout for community needs. They give quilts to police departments, ambulance drivers, the nearby women's shelter, a group home, a homeless shelter, and other individuals in crisis.

Sounds like a great illustration of a "family affair."

Binding Stitch

Arlean's books include *Whimsical Witticisms* and *A Small Town Is Like a Large Family.* Both are available through Arlean. You can find the Rosemores' quilting activities listed on Facebook (www.facebook.com/pages/Quilts-for -Kids/109524832400567), and you can scope out Mary's quilt shop (Mother Originals) at http://quiltshops.blogspot .com/2012/11/mothers-originals-quilt-shop-pequot.html.

You might also consider building a quilting core within your own family. Even persons who don't actually quilt can be involved in cutting, ironing, acquiring fabric and supplies, publicizing your activities, or researching the needs of your community. Why not hold a brainstorming session at your next family reunion?

Photo on page 201 courtesy of Arlean Rosemore. Photo on page 204 courtesy of the Rosemore family.

REACHING GOALS

Eliminating racism and empowering women — the two overarching goals of today's YWCA reflect its mission of support through life's ups and downs. The organization works tirelessly to protect women from domestic violence, to meet women's health needs, and to educate girls and women in the areas of finance and racial justice.

In 1858, women in New York City organized the Ladies' Christian Association, and within two years they had opened a boarding house for female teachers, students, and factory workers. By 1866, new chapters had formed, and the designation Young Women's Christian Association had taken hold.

The YWCA soon established itself as a health-minded club. In 1870 a Boston boarding house installed pulleys on closet doors, allowing girls and women who'd moved there from farms to continue exercising. Only seven years later, the YWCA in Chicago took an interest in medical needs, and it started a visitation program for homebound patients.

As early as 1889, the YWCA opened its first African American branch, in Dayton, Ohio, and the following year opened a Native American branch in Chilocco, Oklahoma. Other remarkable milestones in the YWCA's history also reflect its overarching aims. The YWCA:

- Became the first industrial federation of clubs to train girls in self-government (1908).
- Convened the first interracial conference in Louisville, Kentucky (1915).

- Held the International Conference of Women Physicians, the first gathering of medical women (1919).
- Extended its services to Japanese American women and girls incarcerated in World War II relocation centers (1942).
- Opened its cafeteria in Atlanta to African Americans, becoming the city's first integrated public dining facility (1960).
- Established ENCORE, a program of education, exercise, and support for postmastectomy patients (1972).
- Held Stand Against Racism campaigns in Trenton and Princeton, New Jersey, which quickly spread to thirty-nine states with over a quarter of a million participants (2005).

Through the years, the YWCA has served as a voice of advocacy and progress in women's issues, and the voice will not be silenced. Whether in job training, preschool care, or financial literacy, the Y continues to serve communities across the country and around the world.

One of its most visible programs is its work against violence, and when women find themselves in untenable situations, they often look to the Y. They know they'll find answers and assistance. And they know they'll find shelter.

In Fort Wayne, Indiana, the YWCA's Crisis Shelter for women and children provides help in time of trouble. It offers computer classes and GED training, clothing and personal care items, and assistance in navigating the legal system. All these services benefit its clients, who've been buffeted about in their stormy lives. But sometimes fulfilling a woman's or child's most immediate need is the greatest benefit of all: a bed — covered with a quilt.

The center's quilts come from several sources, like church groups and community quilting clubs. However, a one-time source, Elmhurst High School, left a powerful impression on the center. That's because the Fort Wayne Community School Board had voted to close Elmhurst due to budgetary issues immediately after its class of 2010 graduated.

But students in Elmhurst's basic fashion and advanced fashion classes chose to turn a negative into a positive by using their skills to make quilts. First, the two groups designed and created a Trojan Memorial Quilt as a final gift to the school they loved. According to the *Ft. Wayne News–Sentinel*, "The five-week project was the first of its kind, and each student in both classes was able to make and sew a square onto the memorial quilt."

As a bonus, class members learned new techniques. Sophomore Erica Crebb said the project required stitch-in-the-ditch, which they hadn't tried before. "We all used old and new skills to bring it all together. We were all really into it, and we wanted everything to look nice, because it was going to a good cause," she said. When they finished the quilt, they presented it to Principal Chad Hissong.

The classes' second project — also a way to say good-bye — involved more fabric and more of the community. They made fourteen quilts and pillows for a donation. Their teacher, Beverly Armour-Thomas, offered her students a list of potential recipients. She said the students wanted children to benefit from their work. After studying the list, everyone agreed on the YWCA's Crisis Shelter in Ft. Wayne.

"We're doing something one last time," said Madison Willcutts, a senior in the advanced fashion class. "We do a lot of great things here at Elmhurst, and this is one of them."

Each of the donated items was made in school colors, with fabrics chosen by the students, and included the high school's name stitched onto it. The newspaper article goes on to explain that Debby Beckman, president and CEO of the YWCA, said the pillows and quilts would be given to children in the YWCA's Crisis Shelter. She also noted the historical significance of these items. "We're very fortunate that the class made the decision that our organization would be the recipients," she said. "It will be powerful that the people we serve [will] be involved in that history."

The newspaper photo shows Elmhurst sophomore Brittany Starks presenting a folded quilt to Debby Beckman, of the shelter. Along with Brittany, a group of girls from a variety of ethnicities stand proudly, representing the two classes. They've done good work, and even though they're saying good-bye to their school, they're coincidentally saying hello to something else: those same overarching goals that stand as pillars of the YWCA.

Binding Stitch

If you're a high-school fashion or fiber arts teacher, consider involving your students in a project similar to Elmhurst's

— even if your school isn't closing! You can access information about the Y at www.ywca.org, where you'll find links to local YWCA-sponsored social services. As with any shelter, before you donate quilts, call to learn about the needs and requirements of that particular facility.

9

QUILTING PROS

CHARITABLE INTERESTS

Marie Bostwick loves quilting. She also likes traveling, playing with her grandchildren, watching movies, and enjoying the view from the front porch of her home in rural Connecticut. Oh, by the way, she does a bit of writing too.

Most readers know her as author of the Cobbled Court Quilt series of books. The first book in the series, *A Single Thread*, has been reprinted more than a dozen times. It and one of the sequels, *A Thread So Thin*, were included in Reader's Digest Select Editions. *Ties That Bind* snagged Best Mainstream Novel of 2012 by RT Book Club. Marie herself was nominated for a Career Achievement in Mainstream Novels award by the same organization.

Impressive credentials, to be sure. But Marie's books are more than just good reads. "I'm enormously excited to use my platform as an author," she says. Through Cobbled Court, she entertains and educates her audience. For example, the quilt shop owner in her series has dealt with breast cancer, and a woman in *A Thread of Truth* is running from domestic violence. These characters' interactions can encourage readers to learn more about the issues and reach out to acquaintances facing similar situations.

Because of her renown, Marie can highlight a variety of good causes not only through her novels, but also in her own life. One of her favorites is the National Down Syndrome Society, which has over 350 affiliates and advocates for the value and acceptance of persons with Down syndrome. Marie also supports Freedom Service Dogs, a registered 501(c)(3) organization, which "enhances the lives of people with disabilities by rescuing dogs and custom-training them for individual client needs." One of the few organizations to provide these animals free of charge, Freedom Service Dogs offers lifetime support to its clients.

A third charity that Marie champions is the National Domestic Violence Hotline. This 24/7 operation provides confidential assistance, crisis intervention, and connections to sources for immediate safety for callers in 170 languages. Marie has dealt with the issue of domestic violence in her books, and she hopes her fans will learn more and become supporters as well. One way she does this is by conducting an annual retreat with twenty-five of her closest readers. "We make pillowcases for the Susan B. Anthony Project," she says, referring to a local group that promotes safety, healing, and assistance for survivors of domestic and sexual abuse. Pillowcases, Marie states, can be used for their original purpose or as a suitcase in an emergency. They also function as gift bags at Christmastime.

Since Cobbled Court hit the bookstores, Marie has found another way to support the National Domestic Violence Hotline as well as other charitable interests. She created a line of auxiliary products to complement the books — fabric, tote bags, coffee mugs, and the like. All proceeds are divided among her favorite charities.

But long before her writing career took off, Marie served her community wherever she lived. At age twenty-five she became president of a new chapter of Habitat for Humanity in Georgia. A few years later she managed Promise Keepers seminars in Colorado. When her husband's job took him to Mexico, she served there as volunteer director of development for Manos de Ayuda, a medical mission for the poor. More recently, she has worked on church and civic projects and has served as a board member for Quilt Alliance. She's also made quilts and donated them to Quilts of Valor, Quilts for Kids, and author Brenda Novak's annual auction for diabetes research.

It's easy to see that Marie Bostwick's life as a quilter, writer, and volunteer moves at whirlwind speed. No wonder why, on rare occasions, she likes to slow down, play with the grandchildren, and enjoy the view from her front porch.

Binding Stitch

You can find Marie's merchandise at www.cafepress.com /mariebostwickshop, and you can learn more about her books at www.mariebostwick.com. Here are the charities mentioned: Susan B. Anthony Project (www.sbaproject .org); Brenda Novak's auction (http://brendanovak.auction anything.com/Home.taf); Quilts of Valor (www.qovf.org); Quilt Alliance (www.quiltalliance.org); Quilts for Kids (www.quiltsforkids.org); National Down Syndrome Society (www.ndss.org); National Domestic Violence Hotline (www.thehotline.org); and Freedom Service Dogs Association (www.freedomservicedogs.org). By the way, this last charity appreciates cash donations, of course, but it also accepts items like collars, leashes, and doggie toys. Look for its wish list on Amazon.com. Sharon Wilson, executive director of FSDA, says, "Anything that we don't have to purchase means just that much more money we can use to provide a dog for a soldier."

MONECA'S NEW CAREER

When a stay-at-home wife and mother decides to launch a career, she usually enrolls in college, finishes a degree, or takes training or retraining to hone her skills. Then she sends out resumes and eventually — she hopes — gets her dream job and works her way up the ladder of her profession.

Moneca Calvert followed a slightly different path. True, she took a class for hands-on training, but she didn't bother with the other steps. At least not in the traditional sense.

After her six children had grown and left home, she considered what to do with the rest of her life. The *Los Angeles Times* reports her musings: "I'd done the mother bit, the wife bit. Like so many women I was a closet person. I'm not a joiner, didn't go out much. I mean, with six children?" she says, emphasizing the number of offspring. "So I told my husband, 'I'm going to have a career.' I didn't ask him. It's just the way it was."

When they both got over the shock of her declaration, she had another decision. "I wasn't sure what kind of career I was going to have." She didn't want a cashier's or clerk's job, so she considered becoming a flight attendant. Meanwhile, she took a quilting class in 1982, because she'd enjoyed sewing since childhood and because she wanted to fill some empty hours.

And that class made all the difference. Her work took off like a sewing machine on steroids, while she learned every aspect of the quilting process. Her husband, Daye, at first skeptical, observes with a laugh and a touch of awe, "If it's not moving, she'll quilt it." From the beginning she approached her new career with intensity, making large quilts and small wall hangings — all museum-quality pieces of art. She's won numerous international quilting awards, teaches quilting and design, and holds court in her studio at the historic Riverside Hotel in Reno, Nevada.

She reached this point with a determined plan. Early on, she'd decided to ramp up her work in order to be recognized in the industry. "I knew I had to get known, in some fashion, to make an impact," she says in an interview with *People* magazine. "For me, it was to exhibit in contests, because that's where the editors [of the quilting magazines] see you. That's how you get published, get a reputation."

She started with local and then moved to national quilt competitions, and in 1986 she considered the biggest of all: the Great American Quilt Contest. To commemorate the centennial of the Statue of Liberty and to raise funds for the restoration of the historical monument, Scotchgard offered a prize for the best entry.

Moneca spent almost six months of eight- to twelve-hour days designing and making her quilt, named Glorious Lady Freedom. She admits, "I had calluses on all my fingers." Her quilt depicts the Statue of Liberty standing before a backdrop of a waving American flag, fields of grain, mountains, and the Manhattan skyline. She hoped to create a memorable image. "I wanted it to be instantly recognizable anywhere on the planet. For me, the flag, the statue, and the country all had to stack up on that 6-foot square," she says, referring to the finished size of her quilt.

With a thousand entries in the contest, the quilt faced stiff competition, but she had confidence in her work. "I didn't do this not to win," she declares. And win she did: a $20,000 first prize and instant recognition. "Glorious Lady Freedom," said an art critic, "is one of the most important quilts produced in the twentieth century."

Moneca's quilts don't follow traditional patterns or designs. She begins with a mental image and says, "The hardest part is getting it out of my head — I have pictures in my head — and getting it onto cardboard or whatever. Then the fun begins!" She enjoys pulling fabrics from her shelves and auditioning them for her designs, which she describes as "random-line." Pointing to a wall hanging with flowers, leaves, and other nature-inspired shapes, she says, "No two lines are the same." When making her Glorious Lady Freedom, she used the random-line approach also. "That was my opportunity to do what I wanted to do, without anybody saying 'You can't do that.'" As she has developed her art, she's found a new sense of freedom, and she encourages her students to try the same and not fear being artistic.

Since the dedication ceremony, Moneca's quilt has hung in permanent display at the Museum of American Folk Art in New York City. And the fund-raiser for the Statue of Liberty restoration? The money from entry fees along with that from corporate sponsors added to an impressive overall total. According to a government website, "By March 1986, more than two million individuals, schools, groups, and companies had donated or pledged about $256 million."

As a result, the Statue of Liberty got the facelift she needed, Ellis Island got renovations, and Moneca Calvert got well-deserved respect from quilters everywhere — plus one special individual. Looking back at her early efforts, she recalls, "My husband said, 'This is a complete waste of your time and my money.' Now he's president of my fan club."

Binding Stitch

The Statue of Liberty quilt contest is long past, but you might help on a smaller scale. You can support the ongoing needs of this national monument (www.nps.gov/stli/support yourpark/index.htm) or you can look locally. Is there a statue or monument in your city park? Who takes care of it? Does it need restoring? Call your city hall and ask how you can help. Perhaps you can make a quilt to honor the sculptor or to honor your city, then hold an auction to raise funds for the monument. If you want a closer look at Moneca and her quilting process, see the video produced by the Nevada Department of Cultural Affairs (www.youtube.com /watch?v=QIlEEx-7HcA).

Sources: http://articles.latimes.com/1986-04-24/news/vw-1759_1_lady -freedom/2; http://gao.gov/assets/150/144559.pdf; www.people.com /people/archive/article/0,,20094023,00.html; http://articles.chicago tribune.com/1986-07-03/entertainment/8602170448_1_american-eagle -glass-pieces; http://articles.mcall.com/1985-04-11/news/2477181_1_quilt -unbleached-muslin-pupils.

Niemeyer's Montana

Montana, also known as Big Sky Country, is home to another "big": Judy Niemeyer and her world-famous paper-piecing technique for quilters.

After her introduction to paper piecing in 1992, Judy taught the skill at the quilt shop where she worked, hoping its emphasis on precision would help her students improve their own sewing proficiency. Since then, Judy Niemeyer Quilting, Inc., has exploded across the United States, Australia, and Canada. Recently she developed a certification process, so that more instructors in those three countries could teach her methods.

Many quilt retailers have followed suit, becoming certified shops. This special designation means employees have undergone regular training programs with Judy. They teach Judy's technique of the month, they prepare kits for customers to make Judy's quilts on their own, and they keep Judy's patterns in stock. These published patterns number over one hundred and feature several techniques, such as traditional piecing, curved piecing, strip piecing, and appliqué.

But when quilters think of Judy Niemeyer, they think of paper piecing. Also known as foundation piecing, this method may have taken root as early as the fifteenth century in Italy, though most quilt historians look to seventeenth-century England. In any case, quilters pieced with scrap paper to stabilize the fabric. Today, machine piecers like Judy have ramped up the process and have developed amazingly intricate patterns using simple foundation techniques.

Although many quilt instructors and books address paper piecing, Judy's unique approach appeals to quilters who don't like the excessive fabric waste. She provides templates to use when cutting fabric before piecing. This ensures the proper size for pieces before they're laid on the paper foundation — without leftover scraps to throw away.

If Judy's busy schedule of teaching and developing new techniques and patterns weren't enough, there's one thing more: her interest in giving back to her community. She supports several local organizations. The Somers/Lakeside Elementary School, which Judy's children and grandchildren attended, has received Niemeyer quilts over the years, which the PTO auctions at its winter festivals to raise money for a variety of school activities. Likewise, the Safe Harbor program on the Flathead Indian Reservation has benefitted from Judy's quilts. Safe Harbor, the only housing program for victims of domestic violence in Lake County, held a benefit auction in which Judy's niece, Jody, had donated a Niemeyer quilt. To Jody's surprise, her own husband won with the highest bid and presented the quilt back to her. Now she owns one of Aunt Judy's quilts, Safe Harbor earned a thousand dollars for its program, and the husband became a county-wide hero.

Judy Niemeyer has given one-time donation quilts to a number of other good causes. Examples include the American Water Works Association (AWWA), the largest nonprofit scientific and educational association dedicated to managing water; and Water for People, which helps poverty-ridden communities around the world build and maintain safe water systems. Interestingly, Judy's Crown of Thorns quilt, originally donated to the Montana chapter of AWWA, was auctioned and then regifted to the national organization. There, it was auctioned again, effectively doubling its benefit to the organization.

One of Judy's most unusual donations came via some of her many fans. Her daughter, Judel, explains: "In 2011, we decided to run a one-year charity drive. We announced it on Facebook." Online friends responded with plans to use their favorite Niemeyer quilt pattern and make a quilt for charity. At the end of the year, Judy chose one of those charities — a scholarship fund for a community college — and made an additional quilt for it. Diane Mitchell, of Arnold, California, stitched the winning entry using Judy's Stepping Stones pattern, and Judy added her finished quilt, Indian Summer, to the benefit. "Because of Judy's generosity," says a grateful Diane, "in 2012 we were able to award more scholarships to deserving students."

Judy's generosity seems to go on and on. Her daughter mentions other recipients, such as tornado victims in Illinois and victims of the school shootings in Connecticut. Yet Judy's donations are usually done under the radar. Few people besides those immediately impacted even realize she's made and donated so many quilts.

One thing's obvious. Not only does Montana have a big sky; it seems to have at least one bighearted resident as well.

Binding Stitch

You can follow Judy Niemeyer at www.quiltworx.com. Use one of her patterns to learn the skill of paper piecing and then make your own donation quilt. Check out some of her favorite charities: Safe Harbor (www.safeharbormt.org); American Water Works Association (www.awwa.org); and Water for People (www.waterforpeople.org).

Occasional Quilts

Meet Fran Snay of Burleson, Texas. Her list of quilting credentials is extensive:

- Quilt and appliqué lecturer
- Quilt teacher in small and large venues, such as church retreats, continuing education classes, and quilt shows — including the gigantic International Quilt Festival in Houston
- Maker of quilts displayed at the Texas Quilt Museum in LaGrange, the Texas State Fair, and the International Quilt Festival and featured in books such as *Lone Stars III: A Legacy of Texas Quilts* and *500 Traditional Quilts* plus numerous magazines
- Winner of countless blue ribbons in various competitions
- Longtime coordinator of three annual quilt retreats as well as luncheons for her quilting students
- President, vice president, and board member of various guilds
- Longarm quilter for the public
- Quilt-show judge
- Founder of the Johnson County Quilt Guild in 1998 and current vice president for programs and workshops

Busy is one word for it. Now retired from employment as a secretary, she says, "Quilting has become my full-time passion." Along the way she's rubbed elbows with some of the greats in the world of quilting, including Ricky Tims, Pat Campbell, Jinny Beyer, Eleanor Burns, Libby Lehman, Alice Wilhoit, and Mary Ellen Hopkins. Several of them, she notes, have shared a meal in her home, thanks to her position in the guilds where they were guest speakers.

But she admits this whirlwind lifestyle won't continue indefinitely. After all, she's almost eighty years old. "Eventually I'll have to slow down," she says with a grin. "All I do anyway is with God's blessing of good health."

Like many in her age group, she remembers various bedcovers as a child. "Grandmother was always making quilts, mostly from old clothing," she recalls, looking back at her earliest recollections in Blum, Texas.

As an adult, Fran took up quilting and made a Log Cabin, which she no longer owns. "I gave it to a friend years ago. In fact, many of my first [quilts] I gave away." Through the years she honed her skills by trial and error and a few classes, and today she continues doing what she loves. In her free time she does even more: she makes small and large quilts to give away.

"I do charity giving on a personal level," she explains. She doesn't donate to a particular good cause; instead, she stitches works of art and gives them when a need arises. For example, she tells about the annual quilt retreat for her class at church. "I always have a small quilt on hand to use as a door prize." She decides — in spur-of-the-moment fashion — when to give it away. At this retreat, she points out, the spontaneity makes the gift more special. "It always puts a beautiful smile on faces," she says. "The recipient loves it and considers it a blessing."

In another example, Fran remembers a work of charity

that blossomed into a much larger project. "I found out years ago that our pastor loves quilts." That one piece of information spurred her creativity. "You know what happened next?" she asks. "Within a few years, his whole family had quilts — including the first grandchild! Their hearts were truly warmed — another blessing!"

Fran's generosity occasionally earns more than a warm heart; it might earn tears of joy. "For some reason, I decided to give a little quilt to a young woman in the office of one of my doctors," Fran says. She chose a 47-inch throw in blues, burnt oranges, greens, and pinks, featuring a needle-turn appliquéd

After giving this quilt to someone at her doctor's office, Fran Snay discovered that it was just what the woman needed.

peacock in a tree. She wrapped the gift, took it to the clinic, and handed it to the office manager while checking in. To Fran's surprise, the woman opened the package and started crying.

Moments later, when Fran saw the doctor, he said, "That's the sweetest thing you could have done for her. She's been sad all day. This is the anniversary of the loss of her father."

"Little did I know!" Fran says, looking back on the moment. She'd made that quilt a few years earlier with no recipient in mind. In fact, the peacock had been a castoff from another project. "I'm always making blocks of any sort," she explains. "If I'm not happy with my intended fabric or color, I turn them into something large or small and use them for gifts."

She encourages others to do the same. Almost all quilters have leftover blocks, which can be made into a quilt or wall hanging. The resulting work of art might sit in the maker's closet for months or even years, but eventually it'll find the perfect home at just the right time.

In addition to these "occasional quilts," Fran also encourages group work. She mentions one of her annual retreats as an illustration. "Every year I coordinate the church class in making a quilt for auction at our Spring Fest. This year I asked for two quilts. I select the pattern, then we get together on fabric choices, make copies [of the pattern] for each student, and the work begins." She says the sale of these quilts helps fund the church's international mission trip — paying the way for one teenage participant who could not have gone otherwise. "To date it has been very rewarding," she notes — for her, for the class, and for the beneficiaries.

Fran herself has been involved in international work, and her quilting expertise travels with her. In 2013 she went to Haiti with a church team. "I was asked to go to teach quilting. We were there for two weeks, teaching every day except Sunday." Under her tutelage, approximately forty poverty-stricken women learned to make bag purses and small quilted items to sell. Many Haitians have not yet recovered from the devastating earthquake of 2010, Fran notes. This new skill would help women regain a measure of financial independence. Dubbed the Sewing for Souls group, Fran's class became professionals during those two weeks of nine-hour days. The U.S. team furnished all fabric, tools, and sewing machines, so the Haitian women not only gained skills, but also the means to put them to use in the future.

Through all the teaching and giving, Fran says, she continues to be rewarded, and she finds this true at home as well as overseas. "I've been truly blessed with my quilting in that I not only love it but share my heart as well as my knowledge with so many." She believes in sharing — both her skills and her quilted works of art. As busy as she is, she still finds time to make occasional quilts, which come in handy in unexpected ways. "It seems that a quilt of any size warms the heart," she says.

Binding Stitch

Surely you, like Fran, have a few cast-off blocks somewhere in your sewing room. Why not dig them out today? Look for a unique way to set them together, then make a small quilt — without any recipient in mind. Keep your eyes open in the months afterward, and you'll find someone whose day will be brightened by that very quilt! If you want to see Fran's big quilts, go to www.quiltsbyfransnay.com.

Photo on page 225 courtesy of Fran Snay.

Diane Rose is one independent woman. She travels alone, enjoys ceramics, and cooks. She's even written and published a cookbook. But today she's showing the world her favorite activity: quilting.

With dangling earrings and long brown hair curling about her shoulders, she perches on the sofa of her spacious den. The room, now a crafting center, features a sewing machine on a large table along one wall. Mountains of fabric rest against another. On every piece of furniture she has strewn numerous wall hangings and quilts, allowing Bob Phillips, of the *Texas Country Reporter*, and his videographer to get a good look at her handiwork.

As they talk, her hands stay busy with an appliqué project in her lap. She has a section of a full-size quilt top stretched onto a PVC frame, and she's making blanket stitches to secure the decorative figure to the background fabric. She laughs and shares funny stories with the reporter, all the while never missing a stitch and never even glancing down at her work. That's because Diane Rose is blind.

She developed glaucoma as a teen, and her sight faded completely in 1984. Undaunted, she worked for the next fourteen years as a radio journalist in Nashville, Tennessee. She met, interviewed, and befriended scores of country music's biggest stars, among them Johnny Cash, Charlie Daniels, Willie Nelson, and Ronnie Milsap. She calls them her family.

She enjoyed the radio career, but something wasn't

complete in her life. "I was kinda depressed," she recalls. "It was raining, and I said, 'You know, God, what's the deal here? I don't get it. Where are my talents?'" As she uttered this makeshift prayer, she says she lifted her hands and felt a strange warmth seep into them. Was that a sign from above that she should use her hands for some kind of work?

The answer came soon. "The next day I was visiting a friend, and she asked me if I knew how to quilt." Here's where Diane's smile grows into a full-fledged grin. "I said no, but I'd love to learn." Her friend offered to teach her the basics.

Since then, she's made hundreds of quilts — all pieced by machine. In addition, she machine-quilts some and ties others by hand.

How? First, she gets help from a friend, who chooses colors and quilt patterns and cuts pieces. Diane describes the process with the Rail Fence pattern as an example: "What I do is lay out four pieces of fabric, 12 inches by 3½ inches, side by side." She stitches them together into a square, using a seam guide to the right of the presser foot. This helps her sew a straight line, because she feels the edge of her fabric and keeps that edge next to the guide. Once she has several blocks pieced, she says, "I lay them out so they alternate between vertical and horizontal" — just as a sighted person would. Next she sews them into rows and then into a quilt top.

What about appliqué? Someone else cuts the figures for her, and Diane takes it from there. "I do a lot of appliqué," she says, "and you can feel where the stitch is, because it's smooth against the main part of the quilt, while the part that's not yet stitched is not smooth."

Many of her quilts have a folk-art look, like her geometric crazy patterns or her children's quilts appliquéd with whimsical animals. Others sport patriotic themes. On one, she appliquéd the whole Pledge of Allegiance in big letters; on another, the faces of all the U.S. presidents. She also makes quilts to fit the needs of her customers, who include everyday people as well as more prominent figures, such as Loretta Lynn and former president George W. Bush. She even made a custom quilt for His Royal Highness Prince William and Duchess Kate. Among its large appliquéd figures are a castle in the background, a British flag, and a baby carriage with William and Kate standing on either side.

Impressive, to be sure, but to Diane quilting is not just a way to make a living. It's her avenue of service to others. Since her career took off, groups around the country have invited her to speak. Whether it's at an elementary school in Wisconsin, a quilt guild in Las Vegas, or a senior center in Alabama, she demonstrates her skills and offers a word of encouragement. She gives motivational speeches at quilt shows and shops, colleges, civic clubs, and women's auxiliaries, stating that "whether wealthy or homeless, young or old, souls are heartened by the message of comfort, expectancy, reassurance, and fortitude." Along with her speech, she offers handiwork for sale: potholders, placemats, Christmas ornaments, and lots of quilts.

Does she consider herself handicapped? "No, not in the least," she says with an emphatic shake of her head. To her, blindness is "just an inconvenience. You have to wait for someone else to help you do some things you want to do yourself."

Though independent, she's grateful for that help, which

comes in many forms. A neighbor stops by and searches her stash for the particular color of fabric Diane needs. A friend comes regularly to cut out fabric. Someone else offers a ride to the quilt-guild meeting. And many people — friends and strangers — donate fabric and thread.

Diane particularly appreciates the fabric. "Every piece that is donated is used in some way to make all kinds of quilts," she says. She uses denim, flannel, and other heavy materials, but like most quilters she prefers 100 percent cotton.

When Bob Phillips's interview with Diane aired on the local television station, he had no idea it would grab the attention of the Governor's Committee on People with Disabilities. The video went on to receive the Barbara Jordan Media Award in 2008, because it portrayed a disabled person as independent and productive, and because it focused on the person first and the disability second.

Since that video and award, Diane has traveled around the globe, spreading her message of hope and perseverance and showing her quilts. In fact, she has noticed a parallel between quilts and humankind. "When you make a quilt, you're putting together pieces of fabric to make one whole unit. Our lives are many individual pieces, but they interact to make one world," she says. "And it's a beautiful place."

Binding Stitch

You can help Diane by inviting her to speak at your group or club or by buying her quilts and other products (www .theamazingquilter.com/ministry.htm, or 254-799-7990). If you know a blind person who has expressed an interest in quilting, you might want to purchase Diane's how-to DVD. Or invite a sight-impaired friend to a quilting demonstration where touching is encouraged. Watch the *Texas Country Reporter*'s award-winning video about Diane at www.youtube.com/watch?v=7lfaSmDxVZQ.

QUILTERS SUPPORT THEIR OWN

Sometimes one quilter can inspire other quilters, and that inspiration can create surprising results. Such is the case with Libby Lehman. More than forty years ago, Libby and her mother signed up for a basic quilting class. Since then Libby grew from a traditional handworker to a leader in innovative machine stitching. She won countless awards, and her artistic quilts hang in museums across the country. Photos of her work have appeared in books and international publications.

Her own book, *Threadplay with Libby Lehman* (That Patchwork Place, 1997), garnered a strong following, as did her classes. She taught enthusiastic audiences in Japan, Germany, Spain, New Zealand, Dubai, Malaysia, and numerous other countries and served as a quilt judge around the globe. Among Libby's creations, her quilt known as Joy Ride was chosen by *Quilter's Newsletter Magazine* and the International Quilt Festival as one of the "100 Best American Quilts of the 20th Century."

Libby embraced quilting wholeheartedly since her beginnings in the 1970s. "Making quilts is an utter joy for me," she said. "Though parts of the process can be tedious, the product is always worth the effort. I cannot imagine *not* making quilts. They are an integral part of my life."

Unlike many quilters, she worked on only one quilt at a time — for a reason. "This discipline helps me to focus in on each quilt as a distinct entity. It also cuts down on the clutter, both literally and figuratively." As she sewed, her quilts became her friends. "Part of my creative process involves an ongoing dialogue with my quilts," she explained. That's why she preferred finishing one before beginning another. "Too many voices trying to talk at once would be distracting!" So from start to finish she stayed with a single project and enjoyed the journey.

But everything changed on April 30, 2013. After returning home from a quilt show in Paducah, Kentucky, Libby complained of severe headaches. Her husband took her to the doctor, and while in his office she experienced a ruptured aneurysm. After a dash to a Houston hospital, she endured a seven-hour surgery. A few days later, she suffered a stroke and vascular spasms, which required additional surgery.

Ups and downs followed: rehab, infections, hospital stays, therapies, skilled nursing care. Weeks turned into months on "an uneven road to recovery," says an entry in Libby's Caring Bridge blog.

Cathy Arnold, Libby's sister, states that "a recovery plan is beginning to take shape." Still, she and other family members know the healing will happen slowly and unpredictably. At some point they had to consider finances. Cathy says, "Medicare will only pay for a portion of the cost of the rehab. She does not have an auxiliary policy. The burden of paying for the long-term rehab and care will fall to [husband] Lester and the family."

Thankfully, the quilting community has heard and answered the call. One member of that community is Gloria Hansen, a renowned mixed-media artist. She accepted the challenge and agreed to help. On her blog she says, "Libby is a true superstar in the art quilt world, and she needs our love and support."

Likewise, Ricky Tims, internationally known quilter and teacher, has joined the team. Although he contributes to other charities, he's refocusing. "Most recently," he says, "my support has been going to the Libby Lehman Medical Fund. Libby was one of the brightest lights in the quilting industry until her stroke in May of 2013. She's still on a hard road, and the expenses have been substantial."

Dozens of other quilt artists have taken up the cause, and support has grown far beyond Gloria and Ricky. One impressive example includes a group of quilters on a tour organized by Jim West, founder of Sew Many Places. His company plans trips specifically for quilt enthusiasts, taking them to exotic destinations like Bali and Tuscany. After Libby's medical needs surfaced, Jim set up the Libby Lehman Soul of a Quilter Cruise. The outcome far exceeded his expectations.

In a letter he wrote to Libby, accompanied by a generous check, he said, "I am overjoyed with the results of our fund-raising cruise that we held in your honor a few weeks ago." He went on to praise the generosity of everyone on the trip, including quilt teachers who'd been inspired by Libby: Pam Holland, Dana Lynch, Jinny Beyer, and Sheila Frampton Cooper. His letter concludes with this statement: "You are one of the classiest people I have ever met, and by far one of the most inspirational quilters in the industry."

Elsewhere, quilters organized another kind of fund-raiser for Libby. A collection of unique quilts, created by award-winning artists and inspired by Libby and her patterns, was presented at the International Quilt Festival in

Houston in the fall of 2014. That same collection was then moved seven hundred miles northeast and hung at the American Quilter's Society Show in Paducah the following spring. All quilts were auctioned and sold to the high bidders across the country. One hundred percent of the proceeds went toward Libby's medical expenses.

Her sister, in awe of the support, says, "The family is very appreciative of all cards, letters, quilt pieces, and contributions received on behalf of our beloved sister, Libby. She is a real treasure to all of us, and we all want her to be able to recover to the best of her abilities. Thank you so much."

Looks like the inspiration, begun years earlier by Libby, will continue into the future.

Binding Stitch

As stated above, Libby Lehman's ongoing health issues will require more donations. If you're interested, for updates visit Gloria's blog (www.gloriahansen.com/weblog/?p=8543) or Caring Bridge (www.caringbridge.org/visit/libbylehman/mystory). In addition, you can learn about Jim West's tours at www.sewmanyplaces.com, and quilter Ricky Tims at www.rickytims.com. You can find the 100 Best Quilts of the 20th Century at www.bryerpatch.com/gallery/100BestQuiltsOfThe20thCentury.htm.

You might also want to look closer to home. Perhaps you know of a quilter in your local guild who's facing insurmountable financial problems due to a major health issue.

You could start a website or blog to publicize the situation. You could also set up a bank account for contributions and announce the campaign at your next guild meeting. Why can't *you* be that caring friend who gets the process rolling?

10

EVEN ANIMALS
NEED QUILTS

SEW THE SEEDS

What does the scalloped hammerhead shark have in common with the peregrine falcon? How about the Mojave fringe-toed lizard with the elkhorn coral? Each plant or animal holds a place on the list of endangered or threatened species. Around the globe, scientists have catalogued this ever expanding list from year to year, with no apparent end in sight. What can be done?

Nothing, say observers on one side of the debate. Animals and plants become extinct naturally in many cases, and we must accept this as a normal part of the life cycle.

On the other side you'll find passionate disagreement. These advocates point to human-induced issues, such as poaching, that endanger many species. In Tanzania alone, according to a 2014 article in *National Geographic*, the population of elephants has fallen by 80 percent in just six years. Across the Atlantic, illegal logging in Mexico contributes to the dramatic dwindling of the monarch butterfly. And throughout North America, the number of freshwater mussel species dropped to almost zero due to pearl hunters in the mid-1800s and button makers in the early 1900s.

Shocking statistics, to be sure, but some positives are emerging. First, many countries have enacted new laws and regulations. Examples include increasing fines and jail time for poachers, curbing the demand for ivory, tightening or eliminating loopholes in logging-industry regulations, and encouraging the recultivation of mussel species.

Here's another positive trend: raising awareness about endangered species. When more people around the globe care about this issue, say activists, more will be done to help. And one woman has found a way to increase interest. She made a quilt.

Sherrell Cuneo's deep concern for wildlife developed years ago. "As a child I wanted to be an ornithologist and have always felt an emotional bond with animals and environmental issues." Coincidentally, she became a professional costumer, learning quilting as a hobby and organizing community quilt projects.

In 2012 one animal's death served as the impetus for combining her love of quilting with her love of animals. Lonesome George, a Pinta Island tortoise, had lived about one hundred years and was considered the last of his subspecies. Some experts called him "the rarest creature in the world" and often pointed to him as a prime example of the need for conservation efforts in the Galápagos Islands. Looking back to his death, Sherrell says, "I was saddened by the passing of Lonesome George and felt called upon to do something."

As she considered her options, she recalled the immensely popular NAMES Project AIDS Memorial Quilt, established in 1987. The mission of this project was — and still is — "to preserve, care for, and use the AIDS Memorial Quilt to foster healing, heighten awareness, and inspire action." The NAMES Project comprises thousands of quilt panels, each 3 by 6 feet — roughly the size of a coffin lid — assembled into "blocks" of eight panels each. The huge, fifty-four-ton quilt travels to almost a thousand venues each year, encouraging loved ones to continue stitching panels to memorialize those who have died of AIDS. Sherrell says,

"The obvious parallel with the AIDS quilt leapt to mind and evolved into the idea for Sew the SEEDS."

Sew the SEEDS (Saving Earth's Endangered and Diverse Species), a loosely knit group of teachers, stitchers, environmentalists, and others, started simply. Sherrell made two 3-by-6-foot memorial panels — one for Lonesome George and one for Martha, the last passenger pigeon, who had died in 1914. Since that two-panel beginning, Sew the SEEDS has taken hold elsewhere. Elementary teachers use the concept to teach science, natural history, language arts, mathematics, and fine arts.

Sherrell offers two classes as examples. Linda Harada and Aileen Rabina, teachers at Thomas Starr King Middle School in Los Angeles, kicked things off in the spring of 2013. Their students designed and constructed panels for fourteen species. In the process, they learned about biomes and the importance of food chains. Sherrell adds, "They also researched why each species was endangered, what part people play, and what we can do to help." But the project didn't stop there. "Each group created a minidocumentary and a public-service announcement." Rabina's language-arts class even learned how to write persuasive letters to newspapers and legislative representatives.

This enthusiastic student involvement served to launch Sew the SEEDS. Now Sherrell receives donated quilt panels from schools as well as from individual quilt makers and artists. "We hope that our work will inspire others to make their own panels and share them with us," she says.

She suggests using medium-weight cotton and encourages participants to consider "reused and repurposed fabrics" for an environmentally friendly product. She asks for backing, but does not require batting. Any combination of piecing, appliqué, paint, collage, or photography is acceptable, and Sherrell likes to see photos of the quilt-making process.

Finished panels may be donated by quilt makers to Sew the SEEDS or to an organization of their choice. For example, a Pacific leatherback sea turtle panel now hangs in the Turtle Island Restoration Network office in Olema, California. A panel on coral reefs, still in progress at this writing, will go to the Center for Biological Diversity, based in Tucson. And Sherrell's panel for Martha the passenger pigeon hangs in her local Audubon Society office.

If individual panels like these can impact viewers, imagine the power of several combined. Sherrell says, "The panels done by the students in Ms. Harada's and Ms. Rabina's classes have all been sewn together into full 12-foot square quilts. Each class did seven species, and we finished out each quilt with a panel devoted to pictures of the students at work. I currently have four full quilts made by these sixth-grade classes." Impressive!

Kids who may have had no interest in either quilting or endangered species have found enthusiasm for both —

Quilt panel depicting a Pacific leatherback sea turtle, with plastic bags symbolizing trash that might threaten the species.

especially when they see their oversize quilts on display. Sherrell hopes more teachers will get on board, adding that "we have created a model that can be followed or expanded upon at schools."

Though some may scoff at the giant leap from sixth-grade quilters to nationwide environmental concern, Sherrell begs to differ. "For all their quaintness and coziness, quilts and 'women's' handcrafts have a long history of use as a form of political activism." She cites the AIDS Memorial Quilt as a prime example. Lesser-known instances can be seen in the historical names given to quilt patterns through the years. Consider these: Fifty-Four Forty or Fight, a popular slogan among Democrats in 1846, referring to the conflict over U.S. ownership of Oregon; Tippecanoe and Tyler Too, a reference to the presidential election of 1840; and Lincoln's Platform, promoting the sixteenth president. In every case, "women's work" served as a catalyst for change, activism, and awareness of the issues of the day.

In order to carry on this tradition, Sew the SEEDS needs quilt panels as well as fabric donations. Its website thanks Universal Studios Costume Shop for a gift of "unused and remnant fabric from the movie *47 Ronin*." Sherrell adds that the Los Angeles Center Theater Group also donated fabric, which will be passed along to schools to allow more students to make more quilt panels.

Recognized by the Center for Biological Diversity and by Enrich LA, which establishes edible gardens in urban schools, Sew the SEEDS has, in only a few years, established itself as an organization that truly cares for and educates about endangered species. Sherrell Cuneo hopes others will join the cause. "We use the grand old tradition of quilting, a nexus between art, activism, and community building, to create beautiful fabric panels to be shared, displayed, and used in every way possible to spread awareness of the threat of species extinction."

Recalling endangered species like scalloped hammerhead sharks and peregrine falcons as well as her own childhood love for living things, Sherrell says, "To me this is personal. Somehow, more people need to know about this and become involved."

Binding Stitch

Whether you're a teacher, a homeschool parent, or just a concerned individual, you can get involved! Do a little research to learn about hundreds of endangered species (www.fws.gov /endangered). Next, choose one of particular interest to you, study it, and make a quilt panel to represent it. Be sure to document your creative process with photos. When finished, contact Sew the SEEDS (www.sewtheseeds.org). You can also tell others about this project, inviting like-minded people to join. Go to www.sewtheseeds.org/blog for more information. Learn more about the endangered species mentioned above: elephants (http://news.nationalgeographic.com/news /2014/06/140613-wildlife-trafficking-elephant-poaching -ivory-china-anson-wong-celia-ho); butterflies (http://news .nationalgeographic.com/news/2014/10/141010-monarch -butterfly-migration-threatened-plan); and freshwater mussels (www.fws.gov/endangered/news/episodes/bu-Spring -Summer2014/story2/index.html).

Photo on page 243 courtesy of Sherrell Cuneo.

A QUILT ON THE COUCH

Take one look into his chocolate-brown eyes, and you're a goner. You immediately fall in love, and you want to bring him home to meet the family. You imagine yourself spending a lifetime with him, frolicking on the beach, jogging through the park, settling onto the living room rug with his head in your lap. You can even see yourself brushing his coat and rewarding him with treats when he shakes your hand or rolls over on command.

Yes, your new love is a mixed terrier pup, or maybe he's an older shepherd. It doesn't matter what he looks like or how big he is. Before he met you, he'd been rescued, turned over to a shelter, nursed to health, and rehabilitated. And now he can be yours forever!

That's the goal of the Animal Shelter of Texas County (TASTC). Located in southern Missouri, Texas County and its county seat, Houston, are often confused with counterparts in the Lone Star State. But there's no confusing the animal shelter and its mission. TASTC's website describes lovable dogs waiting to be embraced by families. It also provides heartwarming letters from people who've accepted a new pet, like Bailey's family, the Tates: "We absolutely love Bailey!" they gush. "He is a wonderful dog!"

Such letters make Rita Romines smile. She's the founder of TASTC and president of its board. Years ago, after moving to Texas County, she noticed a problem. "I was always picking up a stray dog or cat, and I thought the area needed something for strays." Deciding to act on her concern, she gathered a few friends and started a shelter, the only no-kill shelter for several counties around. Not only does TASTC rescue cats and dogs; it cares for the whole animal. "We spay and neuter, and we get them all their shots," says Rita.

Founded in 2006, this nonprofit relies on the generosity of its community. Donations of cash, pet food, laundry detergent, trash bags, and other utility items arrive at the shelter regularly. Quilters contribute as well, Rita notes. "People come in all the time, donating bedding for dogs. Our quilters' guild also makes cat beds for us, made from leftover materials. It's a real act of love; they don't have to do that."

TASTC appreciates all such donations. But on one occasion it received something nicer, something that probably shouldn't line the bottom of a cat cage or a dog pen: a brightly colored lap quilt. "I don't even know who made it," Rita says. Perhaps the donor brought it as a thank-you for the shelter's work; perhaps she simply wanted to add a dash of color to the shelter. Rita doesn't

Who can resist a puppy on a quilt? Rita Romines occasionally uses a donated quilt to help promote animal adoptions at the Animal Shelter of Texas County.

know the donor's wishes for the quilt, but the staff came up with an idea. The quilt covers the back of the couch in the reception room and serves as an occasional backdrop for photo shoots and television spots. After all, adoptable puppies and kittens seem more appealing when posed on an appliquéd quilt of reds, yellows, and greens.

But animals, not quilts, are the focus of this organization. In many cases, TASTC finds homes for dogs and cats almost immediately, and the staff rejoices. However, there's a different option — also cause for rejoicing — for certain other dogs. It's a program Rita and the TASTC board have wholeheartedly embraced: Puppies for Parole.

A nonprofit organization endorsed by the Missouri Board of Corrections, Puppies for Parole matches needy dogs with prisoners who train and socialize them for a new life. The dogs in this program come from backgrounds of abuse or neglect, and they require considerable rehabilitation. Fortunately, the benefit is two-way. Board director George A. Lombardi says, "The dogs have a remarkable impact on offenders, improving offender behavior and giving offenders incentive to maintain excellent conduct records. Staff morale is also enhanced by the presence of the dogs."

Thanks to this program, prisoners discover a reason to get up in the morning, and even the most hardened person can feel compassion watching a dog regain health and happiness. Puppies for Parole's slogan says it all: "Rescuing dogs from a lifetime of pain, releasing people for a lifetime of change."

Most of these newly rehabilitated dogs become valued members of families across Missouri and beyond. "We network with shelters everywhere," Rita says. "We've sent dogs to Washington, Connecticut, Illinois." She's justifiably proud of TASTC's long-reaching influence.

But not every dog goes to an out-of-state shelter and joins a family. Some become companions of a different sort, trained to work with the disabled, children with special needs, veterans, and mental-health patients. One example involves a Lab mix named Soldier. After his rehab with Puppies for Parole, he moved into the Missouri Veterans Home in Mexico, Missouri. A staff member tells of a time when Soldier kept watch over an aging veteran throughout the night until the vet's passing. The next day Soldier stayed at his post, comforting the family — even licking away a daughter's tears of grief. That woman later wrote to Puppies for Parole, stating, "All I needed was Soldier to help me, and he did. Thank you for allowing him to comfort me in my time of need — it helped me to deal with the passing of my father."

That's one success story among hundreds, showing why Rita Romines continues to serve the Animal Shelter of Texas County. Such stories encourage donations to this worthy cause — even by the person who lovingly stitched the quilt draped over the reception-room couch.

Binding Stitch

You can find more heartwarming stories about rescue animals at www.tastc.com. If you live in Texas County, please consider becoming a regular donor or adopting a furry friend for your family. In addition, you can learn more about Puppies for Parole at the Missouri Department of Corrections site (http://doc.mo.gov/DAI/P4P.php) or its Facebook page (www.facebook.com/MissouriPuppiesfor Parole). If you live elsewhere, please find your own local shelter to learn its needs and discover how you might become involved.

Photo on page 247 courtesy of TASTC.

Epilogue

Maybe you're a quilter; maybe not. In either case, you've seen how people with a variety of talents and skills can touch lives locally and around the world. Now it's your turn.

Don't set this book aside without a bit of review. Did a certain charity appeal to you as you read? Maybe you turned down the corner of a particular page or left a bookmark there. Did you consider how you could contribute a quilt or supplies or cash?

If so, get busy. Set a goal that's feasible and time-sensitive. Can you make one quilt for that charity by the end of next month? Send a monetary donation? Purchase supplies? Offer to cut or iron or deliver?

I challenge you to get involved with existing charity work, or look at the needs around you and start something new. Then you too will make a difference in your world!

Acknowledgments

"Many hands make light work." My mother's favorite saying certainly holds true for the writing of this book. Even though I crafted each chapter myself, I did so with help from scores of people. An elderly woman in Georgia, a hospital chaplain in Seattle, a nurse in Indonesia, and approximately seventy-five others patiently answered my questions about quilts they'd made or received or purchased. Thanks to all of you!

In addition, I offer thanks to the unnamed and unnumbered persons who designed and wrote informational websites that supplemented my research and helped immensely. Thanks also to relatives, friends, and even classmates from high school who suggested names of quilters for me to interview.

I thank Georgia A. Hughes, of New World Library, and the 2014 San Francisco Writers' Conference, where I met her. Georgia immediately believed in my idea of a book about quilters making a difference in the world, and she patiently and expertly guided me through the publication process.

Finally, I give thanks to God in heaven, who provided me "the pen of a ready writer" (Ps. 45:1) as I completed this book.

INDEX

Index

Index

ABOUT THE AUTHOR

Ruth McHaney Danner lives and quilts in Spokane, Washington. While still a child, she admired her mother's quilting skills, and she made doll quilts with scraps from her mother's sewing projects. As an adult, she began hand quilting, and her work has won numerous awards over the years. Her sewing room overflows with stacks of fabric, bags of scraps, and an endless supply of UFOs (unfinished objects). She always has a hand-quilting project as well as piecework in progress. In the past several years, she's made dozens of quilts for charitable organizations and for individuals in need. She has written extensively for various publications and is the author of *What I Learned from God While Quilting*.